UNSHACKLED

ISBN: 978-1-77995-004-8
e-ISBN: 978-1-77995-005-5

First edition, first impression 2022
Reprinted 2022

Published by Bookstorm (Pty) Ltd
PO Box 4532
Northcliff 2115
Johannesburg
South Africa
www.bookstorm.co.za

Edited by Barry Cohen and Tracey Hawthorne
Proofread by Janet Bartlet
Cover and book design by Dogstar Design Studio
Cover image of author courtesy of the MTN archives
Cover image of Alexandra by Johnny Miller / Unequal Scenes
Printed in the US

UNSHACKLED

**My journey from the
township to the boardroom**

JEFF VAN ROOYEN

BOOK**STORM**

CONTENTS

Foreword   i

Preface   iii

Prologue   vii

PART I: Back to my roots   1

   1. Family   2

   2. Child of the townships   11

   3. Friends and foes   22

PART II: Laying foundations   33

   4. Stops and starts   34

   5. Moving up   43

   6. A brand new world   52

   7. Into business   62

PART III: Building a legacy   71

   8. The big leagues   72

   9. Professional bodies   83

   10. Knowledge sharing through directorships   96

   11. Fit body, fit mind   110

PART IV: Paying it forward   117

   12. Standing up for the caddies   118

   13. Giving back   128

   14. Thoughts at 70 and beyond   142

Afterword   147

References and further reading   153

Appendix I: Presidents of Abasa   155

Appendix II: Awards and citations   157

Appendix III: Business lessons learned   159

Appendix IV: The plight of the townships   166

FOREWORD

It has been my great privilege to have known Jeff van Rooyen for the 15 years he has served with distinction on the board of Pick n Pay. His deep caring for our company and our common belief that 'doing good is good business' have anchored his invaluable contribution throughout.

His remarkable career is a testament to his professional calibre: he was the chief executive of the Financial Services Board, chairman of the Financial Reporting Standards Council and founding president of the Association for the Advancement of Black Accountants of Southern Africa, among many other prestigious achievements. But it is as a man of the utmost integrity who has risen to the pinnacle of the accounting profession and beyond that his story is most compelling. Having faced adversity from an early age, he can attribute his extraordinary success to the strength of his character.

His is an inspiring story of what is possible for those determined to rise above their circumstances. It is a story of courage and hope that should spur readers of this book to greater heights in every endeavour.

Raymond Ackerman
Founder, Pick n Pay
Cape Town, March 2022

ii

PREFACE

*'Dream no small dreams for they have no power to
move the hearts of men.'*

Johann Wolfgang von Goethe (1749-1832)

Apartheid tried its damnedest to shackle me as a black person –
hence the title of this book. Growing up, I experienced real physical
constraints, as well as psychological ones.

We all know that the psychological scars remain long after the
physical barriers have been removed. Even when I was physically
constrained, as I explain in this book, I always tried to keep my
mind unshackled. I worked hard to strengthen my will, resolve
and self-belief. So when I was told that I could not do something
because of the colour of my skin, I would ask, 'Why not?'

Many told me that my dreams weren't possible: my white lecturer in accounting at university in the mid-1970s said that I was
'aiming too high' in my pursuit of chartered accountancy; a white
colleague told me that Raymond Ackerman would never appoint
me as the chairman of the audit committee of Pick n Pay because
he was 'spoiled for choice'.

Writing this book has been a fascinating and rewarding journey.
As I reached the age of 71 years, the process afforded me an invaluable opportunity to reflect on my past.

Many people live a fruitful and productive life in the hope of making a difference to society, even in the smallest way. My life changed quite dramatically for the better when I qualified as a chartered accountant at the age of 31, at least six years behind the average qualifying age. My career then gained traction and I ended up holding significant positions in both the public and private sectors. These included becoming a partner in Deloitte, chief executive of the Financial Services Board (now the Financial Sector Conduct Authority) and of Uranus Investment Holdings, non-executive director of the MTN Group, lead independent director of Pick n Pay Stores and chair of Exxaro Resources. And, thankfully, my life wasn't all work: I was also able to plough back into the community through supporting a number of charitable organisations, some of which I founded.

I've had the privilege of travelling all over the world over the course of my career. I've been to almost every country in southern Africa and to others in north, east and west Africa. I've visited most of the major cities of the world, from Amsterdam to Mumbai and from Rio de Janeiro to Moscow. During these trips, I've visited museums, churches, temples, theatres and monuments, and engaged with people, generally trying to understand local cultures and norms.

In this way, my perspective of people and the world has been broadened, and what's become clear to me is that people everywhere are essentially the same. We have the same hopes, fears, dreams and aspirations. We have the same challenges of war, destruction, exploitation, overpopulation, poverty and deprivation. Many of us worship the same god, even though we may name him or describe him differently.

What has always encouraged me is what I've observed as the strength of the human spirit: we endure, no matter the trials and tribulations; there's always the faith, courage and resilience to survive, to make it through one day and the next.

◆

My life has certainly not been a smooth ride – there were many obstacles along the way – but I was also fortunate in that there were countless people who supported me in one way or another. It's not possible for me to mention all of them in this book but they know who they are, and they know that I will always be grateful for their support.

For the making of this book, I'm grateful to Bernard Fridman, Edwin Jenkins and Linda Saulsby for sharing their recollections; and to Karen Shirley, Koosum Kalyan, Professor Angela Mathee, the late Mashudu Munyai, Reynold Collins, the late Lloyd Theunissen and Mxolisi Mgojo for the interviews that helped refresh my memory. I'm also grateful to Raymond Ackerman for his kind foreword, to Barry Cohen for his invaluable guidance, my daughters Althea Seoposengwe and Cheryl Hart for brainstorming the book title with me, and to Shamila Diljan for her kind assistance with the manuscript.

Jeff van Rooyen
Johannesburg, March 2022

PROLOGUE

In my final year of study for my bachelor of commerce (B.Com) in 1975, I attended the University of South Africa's two-week 'winter school'. Because Unisa was a distance-learning university, this fortnight around the middle of the year was the only time when students saw their lecturers in person. In those days, winter school was conducted on a racially segregated basis, with white students attending the university campus in Pretoria, and black students being taught at high schools in Mamelodi (for African students), Laudium (for Indians) and Eersterus (for coloureds).[1]

Not many coloured students were pursuing a career in accounting,

---

[1] South Africa's racial classifications can be confusing for those unfamiliar with them. Racial classification was the foundation of all apartheid laws, and the Population Registration Act of 1950 placed individuals in one of four groups: 'native', 'coloured', 'Asian' and 'white'. 'Natives' – the majority population – were indigenous black Africans; 'coloureds' were a multiracial ethnic group descended from the intermarriage of white settlers, African natives and Asian slaves who were brought to South Africa in the 18th and 19th centuries, and who spoke mainly Afrikaans; 'Asians' were those with south-Asian ancestry, most commonly descended from people who migrated from British-ruled Indian to South Africa in the late 19th and early 20th centuries; and 'whites' were predominantly descendants of Dutch, German, French Huguenots, English, Portuguese and other European settlers (culturally and linguistically, they were divided into Afrikaans- and English-speaking groups). 'Honorary whites' were granted almost all of the rights and privileges of 'whites', and included (mainly for economic reasons) Japanese and Chinese people. Other 'honorary whites' were the cricketers in the West Indian rebel teams, Maori or Samoan players in the 1970 touring All Blacks rugby team, Australian Aboriginal tennis player Evonne Goolagong Cawley, and African American tennis player Arthur Ashe (although he refused the label, and demanded to be booked as a black man when he visited and played in South Africa). In 2008, over a decade after the end of apartheid, a high court in South Africa ruled that Chinese-South Africans would be reclassified as 'black', a term that now includes black Africans, Indians and others who were subject to discrimination under apartheid. As a result of this ruling, ethnically Chinese citizens could benefit from government affirmative-action policies aimed at undoing the effects of apartheid.

so only two of us were in the classroom where the accounting lecture took place. In order to break the ice, the lecturer, who was white, asked us what our career aspirations were. We both told him that we wanted to become chartered accountants.

To our shock, the lecturer whistled and then laughed. 'Boys, boys,' he said. 'We're not living in Fantasyland here. You've got to have more realistic aims. I myself have tried several times to pass the board exam, and I'm telling you, if I can't make it, you haven't got a chance.'

The 'board exam' was a very tough examination set by the profession's organising body, the Public Accountants and Auditors Board (now the Independent Regulatory Board for Auditors), which had to be passed before you could call yourself a chartered accountant. Articles of clerkship – an internship that puts your theoretical knowledge into practice – also had to be undertaken. Regardless of the lecturer's discouragement, I decided to pursue my ambitions.

I've lost count of the number of times people have counselled me on aiming too high. Most of the time, their advice was that I should lower the bar and set myself what they considered to be more reasonable and attainable goals. During my early years, I thought that their motives were based on envy, jealousy or plain malicious intent.

As I reflected on these events in my later years, I changed my mind and gave those pessimists the benefit of doubt. The invaluable insight I gained was that they were probably trying to give me the best possible advice, but through the lens of their own weaknesses, limitations and ambitions. Put another way, if they themselves lacked the knowledge, courage, confidence and ambition to do what I was attempting to do, it made sense for them to be discouraging rather than supportive.

Thankfully, I've always had the confidence and strength of character to follow my own instincts. I've always had the view that unless I tried something, I would never know for certain whether or not I would succeed.

That said, if, dear reader, as you read in later chapters about the positions I've attained and those with whom I interact, it seems my life has been a charmed road all the way to the top, one stepping-stone after another, I have news for you: it wasn't easy. Despite growing up in previously disadvantaged communities, I had big dreams and ambitions. It almost didn't work out as planned, but, fortunately, I was always able to lean on my spirituality and, with a bit of perseverance, opportunity, and meeting some good people, I prevailed.

I've always been a hard worker. I worked tirelessly to gain the respect of my colleagues and to earn my place on the corporate ladder. I believe that everyone has a place in this world and I claimed mine – unapologetically.

I'm a child of the townships, where the difference between success and poverty isn't wealth, but opportunity. Opportunity tends to come if you remain patient and you're able to recognise it. It possibly happens a few times in your life. Many people miss it. A lucky few are able to see and grab it.

In some sense, the defining years of growing up in the townships prepared me to navigate the complex world of work. It unlocked the qualities that are essential in facing the uncertainty and adversity of life.

What I know for sure is that I succeeded in qualifying as a chartered accountant not because I was special or exceptional in any way. A number of critical factors stand out for me. First, you have to have a strong sense of self-belief – this is crucial, as you will often find yourself surrounded by naysayers. Second, you must have a capacity for hard work – you must be prepared to make the necessary sacrifices and put in the long hours. Third, the road to success is often an uphill climb – you'll need to cultivate patience, determination and perseverance. And, last, when opportunity knocks, you must seize it with both hands.

In my professional life I've been to many schools around Johannesburg to give talks on career guidance, in this way creating awareness of and promoting my profession. Contrary to my own experience growing up, and given our common backgrounds, the students in the township schools have identified immediately. They've been able to see themselves in me – if I could become an accountant, then so could they.

———— ❖ ————

PART I

BACK TO MY ROOTS

If you wish to move mountains tomorrow, you must start by lifting stones today.

African proverb

I

FAMILY

Life in a South African township is often synonymous with violence, crime and poverty. Many children grow up with few prospects. Without support or guidance, it's too easy for young people to end up feeling hopeless. Often, children as young as 12 will drop out of school or be initiated into a local gang or even end up on the streets. Some see violence and gangs as a way of life and a culture. The weapon of choice for most is a gun, and, with easy accessibility, almost anyone is able to get one.

This became part of my reality, growing up in the 1950s and 1960s in the Johannesburg townships of Alexandra, Newclare and then Riverlea Extension. But there was another aspect. Notwithstanding the environment, we lived happy and contented lives as kids. We weren't unduly concerned about the future; we lived in the present. We were all at school and doing reasonably well; our teachers were of the highest quality and the standards were high.

I have truly fond memories of some of my childhood friendships, many of which have endured to this day – we meet up from time to time, attend family events, exchange music or simply hang out. And we reminisce about the past. Memory is strange in the sense that while I remember some things well, my friends often jog my memory about other interesting events I've forgotten. The opposite is also true.

◆

I was born in Alexandra on 18 February 1950 to Frances van Rooyen, then a 17-year-old school dropout, and Patrick Chimpini, about whom I know very little except that his family were originally from Malawi. My mother has since told me that she and Patrick lived together for a few years after I was born, but they'd separated before I started primary school at the age of six, and after my family moved to another area a couple of years later, I never saw my father again. I learned many years later that he was killed in a car accident.

As much as I've tried to push my father completely from my mind, I've never succeeded entirely. Every year during my schooling, the question of where my father was would arise and I would give the standard reply – 'I don't know'. As an adult, the question also came up repeatedly, for example, when applying for an identity document or a passport. I've always had mixed feelings about my father but one thing I'm absolutely certain of is the fact that he represented a negative role model. As a result, my resolve to be a good father to my own children is very strong and there's nothing in the world that could make me abandon my family. This is perhaps the one good thing that I learned from Patrick, albeit in a negative way.

I was baptised in the Catholic church on 1st Avenue, and attended the primary school for coloureds on 2nd Avenue. Prior to being registered there, this had given me some cause for concern: as a child of mixed descent, with an African father and a coloured mother, I was never sure where I belonged, as physically I was more like my black-skinned father than my light-skinned mother. Alexandra was a melting pot of different races and multiple cultures: Africans,

3

coloureds, Indians and Chinese. But although our community was mixed, we were reminded daily of our skin colour because we attended schools reserved for different races. So, for example, while my neighbour and best friend Meshack and I could hang out at home, we were forced to go our separate ways when we went to school.

So would I end up at the exclusively African primary school or the exclusively coloured primary school? I guess that because my birth certificate clearly stated that I was of 'mixed' descent and my home language was Afrikaans, I ended up in the coloured school with no fuss.

Also, when I was growing up, racial stereotyping was common, and it was easy to build suspicion and mistrust among the different racial groups. Stereotyping 'the bushies' (coloureds), 'the darkies' (Africans) and 'the coolies' (Indians) came easily and naturally. Of course, this separation of the races and fostering suspicion were a cornerstone of the apartheid grand design – and it was very success-ful, as we now all know.

Today, almost three decades after the advent of our new democ-racy, however, the manner in which many (certainly not all) Africans, coloureds and Indians still embrace and actively promote racial stereotyping is a source of immense pain and frustration for me. I move in circles where some people constantly malign others and where I often have to rail against their racism and bigotry. This is exasperating and exhausting. These days, I choose to remain silent because I'm at the end of my rope; I am kaput, but do not mistake my silence for concurrence or approval.

While we've broken the shackles of apartheid, many of us are still trapped in the shackles of our minds. And how we love our bigotry and intolerance! How we cling to our racial prejudices for dear life! How we refuse to be persuaded by what Martin Luther King Jnr reminded us: to judge people by the content of their character rather than by the colour of their skin!

At this moment, it does seem that the racists and the bigots have the upper hand, that they are ruling the roost, so to speak. But I steadfastly refuse to be a part of this ugly racism and bigotry. I deliberately choose to embrace peace and love and fairness and justice for all.

I will cling, with all my might, to the belief that there is a better way, that it is possible for all of us to rise above our narrow racial identities and to build a society that is truly non-racial, a society where we respect people for who they are rather than for how they look on the surface.

◆

Frances, who found a job in a factory after I was born, was more like a sister than a mother to me, and I was raised largely by my maternal grandmother, Ouma Elsie. I've been blessed to inherit her wonderful genes – Ouma Elsie passed on when she was almost 89 (she died in December 1994) and Frances turns 89 in June this year (2022).

Ouma Elsie was born in 1906 in Kimberley in the Northern Cape. Orphaned, she married my grandfather, Oupa Hendrik, when she was very young. They had seven children – Andrew, Johnny, Paul, Hendrik, Dora, Frances (my mother) and Minnie. When my mother was 3 years old, in the mid-1930s, the family moved to Alexandra.

When South Africa entered the Second World War at the end of 1939, my grandfather was among the South Africans who went to Egypt to fight against the Germans. As far as I know, my grandfather was a volunteer and, like most black South African volunteers, he probably joined the war because he wanted a job more than anything else. My grandmother told me that on his return, like all the black soldiers who'd fought in the war, he received a bicycle as a reward for his service to the country. Insofar as the colonial laws were concerned, however, everything else remained the same: black soldiers continued to be treated as second-class citizens in the land of their birth. When Oupa Hendrik died in 1947, Ouma Elsie – who never remarried – received a military pension that continued to pay out until she passed away.

In those early years, the population of the township was around 135 000, which included about 3 000 coloureds. Alexandra was one of the few townships in the country where black people were allowed to own property, and initially my father's family owned freehold property at number 200, 2nd Avenue, Alexandra. The property consisted of a large facebrick house, separate cottages at the back which they rented out, and a spacious yard.

Later, when I was living with Ouma Elsie, she rented rooms from African landlords, first at number 66 6th Avenue (where I was born) and later at number 15 7th Avenue. The yards were generous and the buildings well constructed with quality facebrick. There were trees all around and I remember climbing them all the time. As children we had ample space to roam and play. I spent many Saturday afternoons at the Kings Cinema, also on 2nd Avenue.[2]

Ephraim, Frances and Patrick's second-born, arrived in 1953, when I was 3 years old. Patrick abandoned us not long afterwards.

The forced removals by the apartheid regime started around that time, with Africans forced to move to Soweto, Katlehong and Tembisa, and coloureds relocated to Eldorado Park, Noordgesig and Newclare. My family was able to secure two rooms for rent in Newclare. Not long afterwards, the western areas of Johannesburg – Sophiatown, Martindale and Newclare – were declared a 'black spot' in a white area, enabling the forced removal of thousands of people.

In 1960, about a year after we moved to Newclare, my youngest brother, Desmond, was born. His father was Ali Buys, who'd been born and raised in Mara in Limpopo, and had come to Johannesburg in search of a better life. I remember the day of Desmond's birth so vividly: we were all so excited about the new baby, my little brother. Our brotherly love was very strong and powerful, and the fact that we were stepbrothers made no difference to either of us.

Ouma Elsie was the matriarch of the extended family, which included my uncles, aunts and cousins. Her eldest daughter Aunt

---

[2] The Catholic church in which I was christened, the primary school I went to in Alexandra, and this cinema are today three of sixteen designated heritage sites in the township.

Dora's common-law husband, Uncle Mohammed, had come to South Africa from India to make his fortune. They had six children: Amina, Dawood, Ismail, Essop, Soraya and Fatima. When I was 12 years old, Mohammed suddenly abandoned his family and returned to India, leaving Aunt Dora destitute. She and her six children moved in with us, into our two-roomed house in Newclare, so the house was very overcrowded.

Things eased a bit when Aunt Dora moved out to be with the new man in her life, and my mother moved out to live with Desmond's father, Ali. They left my grandmother in charge of all of us kids. Ali's support of my mother was sporadic and unreliable, however, and they separated shortly afterwards.[3] In the years that followed, my mother had other boyfriends but never remarried.

As cousins, Aunt Dora's children and I got along reasonably well, although Amina and I – we were the two eldest – fought all the time over who would do the household chores. I always thought that she chose the easier chores and left the hard work to me.

As I reflect today on how and why we became such a large extended family, I realise that the major contributing factor was our fathers abandoning us when we were young. Living together made it easier for all of us to pool our resources and survive.

Life was hard nonetheless, and it was a constant struggle raising

---

[3] Ali then married a woman called Veronica, whom I got to know as a warm and loving person, and they had two children, Antonia and Quinton. Tragically, Ali and Quinton were brutally murdered, shot and set alight, and the motive for the killing remains a mystery to this day. Antonia and I connected after this tragedy and have had a lovely relationship ever since.

all those children, but my grandmother and the other adults did the best they could. I have a memory from before I started school of Ouma Elsie taking me along to her job as a domestic worker – she must have worked for some decent families, as not many employers would have allowed their 'girl'[4] to bring their grandchild along.

We were poor and lived among poor people – a school photograph taken when I was 10 years old, in Grade 5, shows me barefoot and without a school uniform, as are a number of the other children. Despite our difficult circumstances, however, Ouma Elsie was a kind-hearted and generous spirit, and although we hardly had enough to meet our own needs, my grandmother would always share the little we had with our neighbours when they asked for help, and our neighbours reciprocated when we sought help. I developed an understanding of how the poor often collaborate in order to survive during difficult times.

Ouma Elsie would also always take care of the needs of her family, especially her grandchildren, ahead of her own. I remember some cold nights when she would use her own blanket to cover us for extra warmth. I was too young to understand at the time the sacrifices my grandmother made for our benefit.

I would only work out many years later why Ouma Elsie thought that my future prospects weren't as bright as my brothers' and cousins', and why she over-compensated by loving me and nurturing

---

[4] Regardless of the age of the person, black women working in homes were often referred to by their white employers as 'girls', while gardeners were called 'boys'.

me more and making me feel special. In a colour-conscious society, my brothers and cousins were light-skinned, while I was very dark-complexioned. When I was old enough to wash and groom myself, she would wash me all over again in the hope that my complexion would improve. She also chided me for being in the sun too much and felt it was bad for my skin but I was passionate about soccer and, despite her concerns, I was out in the sun every day.

Ouma Elsie taught me that there is dignity in work, regardless of the nature of the job, and that hard work is essential. She coached me in how to interact with other people: if I came across as disrespectful or cocky, she would speak to me about how to correct my behaviour. So I learned early on that the right behaviour was essential if you hoped to make it in life, especially if the odds were stacked against you.

2

CHILD OF THE TOWNSHIPS

Historically, in white South African areas, the word 'suburb' was used in everyday conversation to describe legally defined residential townships.

The terms 'township' and 'location' were the terms local people used to describe the underdeveloped and racially segregated urban areas on the peripheries of developed towns and cities. These areas were inhabited almost entirely by 'non-white' people. The apartheid government established separate townships for each of the three 'designated non-white' race groups: Africans, coloureds and Indians.

The communities in these townships were socially marginalised and economically disadvantaged by the apartheid regime, leading to poverty and social unrest. Because residents didn't own the land on which their houses were built, the construction of their dwellings was informal, with no access to basic services such as sewerage, electricity, roads and clean water. Plumbing was seldom up to scratch, and with water being vital for everything from drinking and cooking to bathing and laundry, sanitation problems were an ongoing issue. People might have to queue at communal taps and then walk long distances back to their residence with heavy buckets. Water pipes weren't well maintained and often got blocked or burst, causing spills and flooding. Where there weren't any toilets, people had to do the best they could with buckets.

Under apartheid, industry, commerce and nearly all white households, including remote farms, enjoyed secure and reliable electricity connections, while few black townships and informal settlements had access. As a result, people in the townships had to rely on fuels such as wood and coal for stoves, and paraffin for cooking and heating, plus open candles for light – the horror of an untended flame setting fire to a shack and spreading quickly to surrounding homes is one that's still present in South African informal settlements today.

So life in the townships was (and in many cases still is) extremely hard – living conditions were uncomfortable at best, quality of life was poor, crime was rife. The shabby run-down third-world streets were strewn with litter, and angry unemployed people gesticulated at or even attacked police and journalists.

Don't be fooled, though – the mainstream media loves to concentrate on bad news. Because while it's true that there was poverty and restlessness in the townships, what you didn't see in the media was the incredible spirit of resilience and creativity that gave townships their reputation as the 'heartbeat' of South Africa. Townships were always a hive of activity – everyone was in the street chatting late into the evening, front doors stood wide open to receive visitors, and the more industrious souls were still hard at work selling goods and cutting hair. There was never a dull moment!

People on the whole were more than capable of rising to any challenge, and amazing stories of selflessness and generosity abounded: orphanages were run on a shoestring and a prayer by people who didn't have resources of their own, let alone for others; schools were run voluntarily by retired teachers with little to no materials at their disposal; soup kitchens were organised by tireless charity workers for people who might well have had only that one meal every day.

And marvellous was the spirit of entrepreneurship and creativity in the townships. Small businesses sprang up overnight in disused containers, or simply on the street when there were no other premises available – spaza shops, hair and beauty salons, craft markets, restaurants and lively shebeens. Larger businesses boomed in some township areas. And in all of these endeavours there was a bustling, vibrant positivity. In fact, even as some people found financial success and finally had the means to move up in the world, many of them chose to stay in the township and close to their cultural and family roots, rather than move to a more affluent suburb with high walls and security gates.

◆

When I was a boy, after school I would meet up with all my friends to play soccer or listen to music. Soccer in the streets where we lived was a daily event and we played league games over the weekends.

In our community our soccer teams were named after the teams in the United Kingdom; I think that this tradition comes from the colonial era when we were under British rule. In Newclare I played for the junior Arsenal team; we moved to Riverlea before I could make it into the senior Blackpool team.

In Riverlea I started off playing for Valiants, which later merged with the Gladiators. There was fierce competition in the Riverlea soccer league against teams such as City Blacks, Blackpool and Rosebuds. In neighbouring Noordgesig there were Leicester City and Manchester United.

We had truly outstanding players in our team, such as Reynold 'Kudu' Collins, Jan 'Danger' Booysens, Salathiel 'Sala' Roberts and Willie Thompson. In my view, Kudu, who was the captain and could score goals from the centre of the field, was the David Beckham of the team; Willie was our Lionel Messi and Danger was our Neymar.

Short in stature but handsome, Willie was confident and lightning fast, he was a centre-forward and scored loads of goals for the team. He trialled for Orlando Pirates and I don't know why he didn't make the cut, given his natural talent.

I was good at soccer and my team did well in a very competitive soccer league. We met at the coach's house once a week for club meetings and the draw for the weekend's play. I played almost every week.

The coach loved soccer, having been good at it in his younger days. He established the club and managed it extremely well. Tragically, he was knocked off his bicycle one morning when he was on his way to work, and killed. His sudden death created a huge vacuum in the team and it took a long time for us to get back on track.

Dealing with the reality of death was very perplexing and troubling to us as children, and this came even more shockingly close to me when I was 12 years old and two of my classmates, Jakob Segelberg and Aubrey Brownley, were involved in a terrible accident.

As a result of the forced removals, there were a number of vacant houses in Newclare, most of them with wooden floors. Word spread quickly that over the years coins had fallen between the cracks in these floors, and youngsters like myself would get into these houses to dig for the money. On this particular occasion, a wall of the house collapsed, crushing Jakob and Aubrey. Jakob died on the spot and Aubrey was seriously injured.

The principal convened a special assembly the following morning to tell the student body what had happened but there was no counselling to help us deal with the tragedy. Jakob and I had been good friends and had competed with each other academically, and I was severely traumatised by his death and haunted by it for a long time. I recall that many of us attended the funeral in our school uniforms.

◆

In the 1960s, when I was in my mid-teens, my family moved to Riverlea, an apartheid-era low-cost-housing development. The township was surrounded by mine dumps, which was a major health hazard, exposing residents to lead and arsenic, especially when we swam in the dam. In the early years, there was no electricity and residents had to rely on candles, paraffin lamps and coal stoves for our energy needs. There were no bathrooms and toilets were outside in the yard.

My mother's younger sister, Aunt Minnie, and her husband, Uncle Danny, stayed behind in Newclare. I spent most weekends at their house so that I could continue going to the cinema (there were two cinemas in Newclare and none in Riverlea) and listening to Uncle Danny's great music collection.

There was also no high school in Riverlea, so we had to commute to Chris J Botha (CJB) in Bosmont, about 10 kilometres west of Riverlea. I'd realised when I was about 13 years old, in Grade 8, that education was the key to achieving my goal of breaking the cycle of poverty, and for this reason, from this point on, I pursued education as if the devil were chasing me.

CJB was named after its first principal, Chris Jan Botha. He was succeeded by Frank Jacobs, supported by Reggie Feldman as vice-principal; Reggie was also my English teacher and, on Frank's retirement, succeeded him as principal of the school. My other subject teachers were Brian Theron, who taught commerce and was also a mentor to me; Herbert Hilton, who taught accounting; Abraham Oliphant, teaching science; George Smith in Afrikaans; Monty Hoskins, who taught geography; and Reginald Herman in mathematics. I have no doubt that if apartheid had not limited their career options, many of these teachers would have soared to great heights in the corporate world or academia. However, despite being artificially constrained in this manner, they never displayed any bitterness or frustration. Rather, they were fully committed to their jobs, and it's clear that they had high hopes for my generation having more options and access to greater opportunities.

I'd been at Newclare Primary School with Sala Roberts, and he also went to CJB; we matriculated at the same time. The Robertses owned successful fruit and vegetable stores in Newclare and Western

Township, plus they owned property and a number of vehicles for the businesses. (I often wonder how much more successful the family might have been if not for apartheid – black people weren't allowed to own businesses or even acquire property outside of the townships, which created an artificial limit on potential business growth.) I remember Sala driving a truck when he was no more than 15 – he was so small you could hardly see him behind the steering wheel.[5]

Willie Thompson was like a brother to me. He always dated the prettiest girls who wouldn't give the rest of us the time of day; in some ways I think that this popularity cost Willie, as girls were a distraction to him, and he didn't apply himself to his school work as he should have. Still, Willie was the first among us to secure a good job, at Gallo Records, where he worked for many years. All of us benefitted from this because Willie built up an outstanding collection of music.

Clive Fortuin was one of my closest friends at high school and we both played soccer for the local teams; I was a midfielder and Clive a goalkeeper. He worked as a barman in the neighbouring township of Coronationville on weekends and made enough money to buy his own car, a Volvo, while he was still at school. Charming and

---

[5] Sala and I both moved to Eldorado Park, where we spent a great deal of our adult lives. He left the family business and worked as a salesman for a number of wholesale companies. Sadly, he lost his wife, Matilda, when she was in her early 50s. In February 2020 I celebrated my 70th birthday by going on a golf tour for a week to Cape Town with friends, including Sala – the trip remains one of my fondest memories of him and it was an incredible blessing for both of us. Sala and I played a round of golf at least twice a month until his death in July 2021.

irresistible to women, he was very particular about his appearance and his dress was always impeccably smart-casual – his nickname was 'Styles'. When we were studying for our matric exams, I would study at Clive's house because they had electricity. Afterwards, often late at night, I'd cross the bridge over the railway line to get home, keeping a sharp eye out for the gangs who used to hang out there.[6]

Some of the other schoolmates from CJB with whom I remained in contact include Lance Mooi, a keen golfer; Lynette Mooi, my co-trustee on a number of charitable foundations; Denzel Bennett, an aspirant golfer and another co-trustee; Richard Page, a keen ultradistance runner; and Mercy Riechel, Charlotte Steeneveldt, Shereen Rayners and Gail Merckle.

◆

As teenagers in the township, our lives revolved around school, soccer, gambling and music. When we were a bit older, we started taking an interest in girls, which brought yet another exciting dimension to our lives.

When I started my first romantic relationship, my good friend Ernest 'Dups' Jacobs was my confidant. He had a bit more experience than me and guided me. As a result he also got to know my

---

[6] Clive went on to teachers' training college and we drifted apart although I did attend his wedding. Many years later I heard he'd got divorced, left teaching and bought a stake in a hotel in Fordsburg, where he worked as the manager, living in a flat above the hotel. One night in 1994, the hotel was broken into and Clive was killed during the burglary. Clive was a peace-loving man and well liked, and it's unbelievable to me that such a good-natured and even-tempered person could come to such a tragic end.

girlfriend at the time very well; she liked him and they got on well together. Dups had a slight stammer and tried to compensate for this by speaking very fast, which made him difficult to follow – but that didn't bother him one bit.[7]

We loved jazz and blues and would hang out at Willie's house listening to all our favourite artists – Aretha Franklin, Diana Ross, Gladys Knight, Roberta Flack, Percy Sledge, Otis Redding, Arthur Conley, Gene Ammons, Hank Crawford, Coleman Hawkins, Herbie Mann and Jimmy Smith. We also fancied ourselves as great singers, which – perhaps with the exception of Paul Molefe – we weren't.

Paul was one of my best friends from those early years in Riverlea. For some reason known only to him, Paul initially introduced himself to us as Patrick and only corrected this much later on in our adult life. Paul was a much better soccer player than me and I always made sure he was on my side. He was competitive and would show anger or exasperation when we made stupid mistakes (and also when we sang out of tune). Paul, who struck me as highly intelligent, had dropped out of school and I encouraged him to go back. Fortunately he did, and went on to build a successful career in the corporate sector as an information technology (IT) expert.[8]

Another friend, Lesley Abrahams, was like a younger brother to me. Les's father, Uncle Abe, was an avid jazz fan and he had

---

[7] Sadly, Dups succumbed to the temptations of alcohol, which was always around us. He struggled with addiction for many years and it would eventually cause his death.

[8] Many years later, when he was semi-retired, Paul was a tutor in a community college. I lost contact with him in 2019 and suspect that he may have passed away.

a huge collection of albums including the likes of John Coltrane, Duke Ellington, Count Basie, Ella Fitzgerald, Louis Armstrong and Mahalia Jackson. Les and I would often hang out in the afternoons listening and dancing to jazz.

We also enjoyed the movies. We would walk from Riverlea to Newclare to go to the Reno and Lotus bioscopes. On weekends, there were special buses to the Lyric and Majestic in Fordsburg. Westerns and action movies were our favourites. I still have a collection of classics – *The Bridge on the River Kwai*, *The Guns of Navarone*, *The Magnificent Seven*, *The King and I*, *Where Eagles Dare* ...

I started gambling on street corners around the age of 12. We played spinning, basically a 'heads or tails' coin betting game. Almost everyone cheated, and unless you took your chances, you'd get cleaned out every time.

From about age 15, I graduated to rolling dice – placing bets on lucky numbers (ours were 7 and 11). The kids roll dice in the townships to this day – take a drive through Alexandra or Riverlea on any day of the week and you'll observe this. They do this not only to make some money but also to relieve boredom.

Depending on the money available, playing spinning or dice could last for several hours. It was fun but could also be dangerous if you were caught out or suspected of cheating or sometimes just because someone was a bad loser.

When I got to matric, I realised that gambling wasn't a productive use of my time. Besides, I never had gambler's luck and lost my money more times than I won. I also felt that it was important to focus on my studies at that crucial time of my schooling. It was hard to break the habit but the fact that passing matric was so important to me helped me to do so.

I've since stayed clear of any form of gambling – I can count on one hand the number of times I've even played the lotto or bet on horse racing. Most of my golfing mates have no interest in placing bets on our games and we play for fun. On those rare occasions I play with golfers who may insist on placing small bets 'to make things interesting', I go along with it out of politeness and then give my winnings to the caddies.

3

FRIENDS AND FOES

As a young man I had numerous encounters with the police who routinely patrolled the townships simply to harass us. Their mandate was certainly not to serve and protect. They would often drive their police vans at full speed towards us in the streets, then brake hard with tyres screeching.

As soon as we had sight of them, we'd take off running like crazy in different directions, jumping over fences or sometimes running right through people's homes – in the front door and straight out the back. There was no point in trying to hold our ground in the hope of having a polite conversation with them. They were out having fun and entertaining themselves at our expense.

As I reflect on these encounters today, I realise how fortunate we were that we weren't shot at and killed as we ran away.

In 1966 I was in Grade 11. Life was hard, and to try and make ends meet, I sold newspapers – the *Sunday Times, Sunday Express* and *Sunday Tribune* – on Saturday night and into the small hours of Sunday morning. The pay was a fixed commission per newspaper sold, but buyers could be generous with tips, which often came to much more than the commission earned.

We'd pitch up at the CNA distribution centre in Eloff Street Extension on Saturday evenings around 6pm, and the boss would distribute the 'corner sheets' that designated your location for the evening. Some of these locations were more profitable than others, with lots more people buying the newspaper at busy intersections. The transport would then drop us off on our corners early in the evening.

My favourite location was on the corner of Oxford Road and Tyrwhitt Avenue in Rosebank. It was popular as there were two cinemas in the area, one along Oxford and another along Tyrwhitt, and sales would be brisk when the patrons came out of the evening show.

I worked out a little trick to get bigger tips out of customers that basically involved taking my own sweet time to find them change – often customers just wanted to get home, and rather than wait while I apparently hunted through my pockets for the right amount, they'd tell me to keep it. But on one occasion a youngish customer looked at me quite intently as I was going through my routine. 'I know exactly what you're doing,' he said.

I looked at him, shocked.

'If I grab you by your feet and hold you upside-down and shake you, I have no doubt that plenty of the right change will fall out of your pockets!' he said.

I found him his change double-quick, and abandoned playing tricks on my customers from then on.

In the early hours of Sunday morning, hopefully with all our newspapers sold, the transport would come to fetch us and take us back to the distribution centre. Finally, around 2am, once we'd got our pay, I'd walk the 10 kilometres to Johannesburg Station. The train arrived at Langlaagte Station at 3.30am and from there it was another 10-kilometre walk home to Riverlea Extension.

One evening, our selling done, I was walking to Johannesburg Station with some friends when a police van came screeching around the corner. We stopped to see what the fuss was all about. Two policemen, or 'gatta', as we called them, jumped out of the van and headed straight for us. We froze.

They demanded to know what we were doing in town at that time of the morning. We tried to explain that we were on our way home from work but they accused us of lying – they said we'd been breaking into shops and stealing goods.

'Ons gaan om die blok ry, en as ons terrugkom moet julle weg wees,' one of them said – they were going to drive around the block and when they returned, we'd better be gone.

We walked on, Johannesburg Station still our destination, but within minutes the van came screeching back. Panicked, we all took off in separate directions. I was running for dear life, my feet hardly touching ground. To my horror, I heard dogs barking. Turning as I ran, I saw two police dogs closing in fast. Within seconds, they were on me, biting me while I squirmed and rolled on the ground, trying to protect myself.

I heard the policemen call off the dogs, which reluctantly let go of my right leg and trotted back to their masters. The men roughly picked me up and shoved me into the back of the van before putting the dogs in a separate enclosure. As we drove off, the dogs were still baying for my blood.

'Wat het ek gedoen?' I asked in desperation – what had I done?

'Ek is net op pad stasie toe. Ek doen niks verkeerd nie.' I repeated that I was just on my way to the station after work, and that I'd done nothing illegal.

The cops ignored me, driving around seemingly aimlessly while discussing what to do with me. The dogs continued barking. The injuries I'd sustained – the dog bites and the scrapes and bruises from being rolled roughly around on the pavement – were making themselves felt, and I was beginning to get frightened. I didn't know if they were going to lock me up or worse. I again pleaded with them to let me go.

Then, suddenly, for no reason I could discern, they took pity on me and dropped me at the station, just in time for me to get my train. I was relieved to see that my friends had all made it to the station unscathed.

As we watched the van drive off, with the cops in the front seat laughing and chatting, and the dogs in the back glaring out at us with their wolf-like eyes, I wondered what it had all been about. Had they just wanted to scare me, to show me who was boss?

Obviously, I never reported the incident. Who would the police have believed? Me, or their brothers in blue? And even if they had believed me, I knew they'd never have prosecuted their colleagues.

◆

If it wasn't the police harassing us in the townships, it was the gangs. In the townships, gangsters were referred to as tsotsis – mainly unemployed youngsters who fought each other over territory and women, and who were openly violent. Extortion, robbery, rape, grievous bodily harm and even murder were their hallmarks, and few ordinary residents dared to walk the streets at night – the townships had no electricity and it was pitch-dark after sunset, one of the reasons Alexandra became known as 'Dark City'.

I remember the adults in my family talking about how they sometimes had to run for their lives on their way home from the Plaza and Kings cinemas at night. Life was cheap in the townships, and it wasn't unusual for me and my friends to come across corpses covered with newspaper on our way to school in the mornings – the aftermath of the previous night's violence.

Interestingly, the playbook of the gangs in the townships back then is no different to what I've observed in the corporate world and in politics. Gang leaders had strong leadership qualities – they knew how to set goals, plan action, inspire, motivate and incentivise their members; and they led from the front, often putting themselves in grave danger. If they'd had better opportunities – education and jobs – these qualities would have propelled them to the top.

I've always had the conviction that having survived the violence of the townships, I could survive anything. In the townships I picked up the knowledge, skills and experience to navigate difficult situations. However, unlike in the township gangs, where conflict is often life-threatening in general, usually the worst thing that can happen in politics and in corporate life is that you can get fired.

One of the most feared gangs in Joburg at the time was Sherief Khan's. Gang member Dan September – 'Bra Dan' – lived in my neighbourhood in Riverlea. Reputed to fire a shotgun from under his coat when circumstances demanded it, he worked at the Majestic cinema as a kind of security guard. He was very tough, and he was feared. But despite his links to Sherief Khan, Bra Dan had a reputation in the township as a true gentleman. Soft-spoken, polite and always well-dressed – a hallmark of Sherief's gang – he never threw his weight around or interfered with the local residents.

In Riverlea, there were also a number of small-time gangs. None of these came anywhere near the status or power of the major gangs but their motto seemed to be 'live fast and die young' – they often found themselves in situations of fight or flight and, depending on the odds of coming out victorious, they would either stand their ground or run and live to fight another day. This wasn't cowardice but a pragmatic choice in the circumstances. Their leaders were often in and out of jail, and what I know for sure is that incarceration conditioned them to become even more hardened criminals. Because the gangs took on the persona of their leaders, when the leader was incarcerated or killed, the gang usually fizzled out.

The three most prominent gangs in Riverlea when we lived there were led by Rodney 'Spotty' Hall, Mapiks Nortjie and Monty Dirk 'Dirkie' Symons. These gang leaders shouldn't be characterised as all bad, with no redemptive qualities. They had simply been forged under the jackboot of apartheid and in an environment characterised by poverty and high levels of unemployment. All three of them were rumoured to have killed at least one person but this remains unconfirmed.

Spotty came from a large family of 11 children, nine boys and two girls. They lived in Lena Street. Spotty's father, Maxi, was a member of Sherief Khan's gang. When Spotty was about 18 years old, his parents got divorced. Spotty was aggressive and short-tempered; no doubt he had lots of enemies but he never bothered or threatened my friends and me in any way, and we always greeted him when we saw him. He was viciously attacked and killed by a group of guys on a corner very close to his house.

Mapiks lived with his family in Riverlea Extension. He always had a stern expression on his face, a warning that he wasn't to be messed with. His gang of about five included Percy 'Dougie' Solomon. Dougie and I both lived in Molopo Street, a stone's throw from each other, and we disliked each other intensely. Dougie was later shot and killed close to his home by a policeman based at Langlaagte Police Station. There was no investigation, which isn't surprising. Although I didn't like Dougie, this saddens me tremendously – no-one deserves to die so violently.

All Mapiks's gang members were always armed with pangas or knives, a favourite being a knife called an okapi. Mapiks was often in and out of prison. Miraculously, he survived this tough environment, got married, had children and eventually died of natural causes.

I had no interest in joining any of the gangs although I did dress similarly to them – Ayers and Smith cap, Arrow shirts, Libro pants, multicoloured rubber belt, Pringle jersey and cardigan, and Hush Puppy shoes. This stance put me in the crosshairs of the gangs, and

I always had to be mindful of where I went. On those rare occasions when I felt particularly vulnerable, I carried a knife for my own protection. As it happens, however, I wasn't carrying a weapon the day my friend Les and I were walking down Kariega Street, minding our own business, and we ran into Dougie who, on seeing us, immediately started a fight with Les.

Les was a quiet and reserved person, and had almost certainly never been in a physical fight.

'Leave him alone,' I said to Dougie. I wasn't afraid of him and felt that I could take him down if necessary.

A brief look of surprise flitted across Dougie's features before his expression hardened and he drew his knife.

Dougie approached me, slowly and threateningly, tossing the knife from hand to hand. Backing away from him, I looked around for any object I could use to defend myself. I spied a big stone and quickly picked it up.

Dougie kept coming, twice stooping to scrape his knife on the ground, a scare tactic. I watched him closely and, as he bent down to scrape the knife a third time, I hit him hard on the head with the stone.

He hit the ground like a sack of cement, this knife skittering out of his hand. I was angry by then, and moved in to finish him off, but some bystanders who'd gathered to witness the spectacle intervened and restrained me. They talked some sense into me, and Les and I agreed to be on our way.

I soon forgot about this incident and felt that Dougie had learned his lesson and wouldn't bother us again. I was wrong.

A few weeks later I was walking home from visiting my girlfriend down Molopo Street when I bumped into the whole gang – five of them, including Dougie and Mapiks. As soon as Dougie saw me, he gave a shout, drawing his knife and running towards me. Before I could react, he and his gang buddies were on top of me, and in that moment I thought that my life was over.

'Hey!' a voice suddenly called. It was Mapiks. He looked at both of us, Dougie and me, and then said, 'Enough is enough. It's time to settle this. Where's your knife?'

Realising he was addressing me, I told him I didn't have one. Without a word, he handed me his. It was big and heavy – certainly bigger than Dougie's. I weighed it uncertainly in my hands – did I really want to stab someone?

My dilemma was solved when Dougie, realising he wasn't going to be able to beat me in a fair fight, suddenly took off running. Instinctively, I gave chase.

Dougie ran in the direction of his home, with me hot on his heels. At his house, he tried to jump the rickety wire fence around the yard, and ended up falling over it just as I reached him. Looking down at him, sprawled in his front yard, I pointed the big knife at him. 'I'll kill you next time,' I said.

I casually strolled back to the gang and handed the knife back to Mapiks. From that day onwards, I had no further trouble from Dougie or from any of the other gang members. I had earned their respect.

'Dirkie' Symons came from a family of five and they lived in Lion Street. One of his best friends and a gang member was Lenny Rosenburg, who had only one arm (we never knew when and how Lenny had lost the arm). When Lenny was by himself, he was harmless, but whenever he was with Dirkie, he was fond of throwing his weight around. Dirkie's family remember him as a loving person, and he was certainly one of the best-dressed guys in town. However, there's no doubt that he had a violent side to him and he had many enemies.

Once, Les and I were gambling near the local shops along Colorado Drive, just off Juma Street. We were playing cards with a group that included Lenny – we weren't afraid of Lenny and felt we could take him down if necessary. However, we seriously underestimated how tight Lenny and Dirkie were.

Les and I had perfected how to cheat at cards and always dealt each other a winning hand, so we were consistently coming out on top. Lenny suspected that we were cheating but he couldn't figure out how we were doing it. Finally Lenny, irritated, left. We thought nothing of it but about half an hour later I heard Les say, 'Here comes Dirkie!'

When I looked up, I saw Dirkie and Lenny running towards us with pangas in their hands. Without a further word, Les and I took off, running along Colorado Drive in the direction of Les's house in Flinders Street. Luckily for us, Les's father, Uncle Abe, was home as we crashed through the door. Within seconds Dirkie and Lenny ran up to the doorway, which was blocked by Uncle Abe.

'Now, now, boys,' Les's father said, quickly sizing up the situation and realising that Dirkie would have to be placated. 'What's going on here?'

'Don't get involved, Mr Abrahams,' Dirkie said. 'Those boys have cheated and stolen money from Lenny, and now they must pay the price.' He pointed his panga at us, over Uncle Abe's shoulder. 'I'm going to cut them into pieces!'

We could see Dirkie meant it, and we were scared. But Uncle Abe kept talking to the furious gangster in a low voice, and finally some rand notes exchanged hands. Dirkie, somewhat mollified, left, with Lenny on his heels, but as he reached the yard gate, he turned and shouted, 'You'd better watch you, you two! I've got my eye on you! This isn't over!'

That was probably the closest encounter I've had with death, and Les and I always bowed and greeted Dirkie and Lenny multiple times from a distance whenever we saw them after that. They would just wag their fingers at us and show that they would cut our throats.

Dirkie was shot to death some years later by Dan September at a club in Fordsburg. Lenny's fate is unknown.

PART 2

———— ❖ ————

LAYING FOUNDATIONS

However long the night may last, there will still be a morning.

African proverb

4

STOPS AND STARTS

When I was in my final year at school in 1967, my teachers rated me as 'most likely to succeed'. One of the top students, I had an excellent academic record. I was hard-working, disciplined and committed to my studies.

It was during that year that the school inspector came around to our school for a chat with us about our career aspirations. I sat with my fellow pupils in a row in the principal's office while he asked each of us, 'What do you want to do when you leave school?' Most of my fellow students said that they wanted to become teachers – this was what the inspector wanted to hear, and he nodded approvingly as they spoke; a few said they hadn't decided yet.

When my turn came I said that I wanted to become a doctor, an early ambition of mine based on what I perceived to be a high-status and well-paying profession. I was good at mathematics and science, and I had the confidence that I could do it.

The school inspector looked quizzically at me and said, 'Why don't you try teaching instead?'

In my first year out of school, what I wanted to study was moot – college or university was simply out of the question as the money wasn't available; and, anyway, because of apartheid we weren't allowed access to any of the universities in Johannesburg – they were all reserved for white folk. Scholarships for a career in teaching were available but, although I've always had the highest regard and respect for the teaching profession, I honestly had no interest in making it my career.

Most of my fellow students did indeed go on to teachers' training college and built strong careers for themselves. Some of them became successful doctors, dentists, pharmacists and businessmen. Some built successful corporate careers, particularly in the IT sector. Others pursued careers as artisans in engineering and furniture manufacturing.

But my own career floundered – indeed, I had no career. For the first two years after matric it seemed as if I was the *least* likely to succeed. I was envious of my classmates who were well on their way to building successful careers while I had no clear direction.

So I searched for a job – anything I could find. My first was in an engineering firm as a machine operator; this was followed by stints as a despatch clerk in a stationery manufacturing company, a filing clerk in an insurance company and a general clerk in a municipality. Over those two years, I squirrelled money away, saving for the day I could finally study towards a degree.

One disturbing incident stands out for me from these years. It was while I was working at the stationery manufacturing business, which was based in Triomf, west of Johannesburg. Triomf had particular resonance for many of us, as it had previously been called Sophiatown – our spiritual home and the centre of our entertainment talent like Miriam Makeba and Hugh Masekela. Africans and coloureds were forcibly removed from Sophiatown during 1959 to make way for whites. Triomf is Afrikaans for 'triumph' – the apartheid state clearly felt victorious following the forced removals.

When I was appointed to the position of despatch clerk at the stationery manufacturer, I was provided with a comprehensive manual of the company's products to study. This manual was my constant companion as I familiarised myself with the products. I was a quick learner and within weeks I was able to satisfactorily fulfil customers' orders.

One morning, about two months into the job, my boss came to the storeroom where I was sitting at a small table, doing my work. He was accompanied by a large sad-looking white man in his 40s, whom he introduced as the new storeman and my new direct boss.

This man struck me as a poor person who'd had a tough life. I never got to know what his qualifications were but it soon became apparent that he had some experience. It was my task to teach him about the company's products and the nature of my own job. I suspected that he resented me because I came across as confident and knowledgeable, and I worried that our relationship was going to be a difficult one.

One day he brought his son, a youngster of about 6, to work with him. When I tried to have a friendly conversation, the young boy threatened to bliksem (beat) me. It was a completely inappropriate reaction to a genial overture, and I realised that the boy felt he had the right to address me, a person many years his senior, this way because I wasn't white. He could only have learned this from the adults in his life, and it struck me that my new boss was a racist.

It didn't take long for my new boss and me to have our first serious altercation. I usually left work around 5pm, as I was dependent on public transport and it was a brisk 15-minute walk to the bus stop where I would catch the 5.30pm bus home. On this particular day, as I was about to leave, my boss asked me where I thought I was going.

'Op pad bus toe, meneer,' I told him – on my way to catch the bus. I refused to call him, or anyone else, 'baas' (boss), as I felt it implied that they owned me, and I wasn't a slave. They resented being called 'meneer' (sir) but I persisted.

'There are still orders to be filled,' he snapped back at me. 'They're due for delivery first thing in the morning. Who do you think is going to do those?'

This was the first time such a situation had arisen, and I wasn't even sure I believed him about the outstanding orders. My immediate instinct was to be defiant. 'No,' I said. 'I must go now so I can catch my bus.'

My boss moved in front of me, blocking my path with his huge frame. 'You want me to bliksem you?' he thundered.

I couldn't believe what was happening, and my outrage made me stand up for myself. 'Go ahead and do it!' I said to him, before stepping quickly around him and making for the exit.

Coward that he was, he backed off. But that wasn't the end of the matter.

One morning, not long after this standoff, I was already at work when he walked into the storeroom. His office was on an elevated platform, and he climbed up the stairs, removed his jacket and hung it over his chair. He picked up some papers from his desk, came down the stairs and left the storeroom, presumably to go to the main office.

Twenty minutes later he was back. He climbed the stairs to his office again, put on his jacket and left.

There'd been no communication with me during this time, and I silently carried on with my work.

About an hour later, I saw him coming towards the storeroom from the direction of the main office. He was accompanied by one of the senior bosses and two white men I didn't recognise.

Storming into the storeroom, he shouted at me, 'Who was here this morning while I was out?'

It had been a fairly busy morning, and three of my African colleagues had helped me execute some orders. I promptly provided their names – I had no reason not to.

'Find them!' my boss snapped.

Two of the men were in the storeroom with me at the time, and the third we had to find in the factory. When we were all together, the senior boss explained that the two men with them were police detectives from the nearby police station. My boss claimed that he'd brought his rent money with him to work that morning, in the inside pocket of his jacket. He said that earlier, when he'd come and fetched his jacket and then gone to the rental office to pay over the rent money, he'd discovered that the money was gone.

'One of you stole it!' he stated, staring at each of us in turn.

I stared back at him, nonplussed. I'd been in the storeroom the whole time, and I knew for a fact that the only person who'd gone up the stairs to his office was my boss himself. Why was he making up this story?

'I promise, sir, we did not take your money,' I said.

The detectives were hostile. 'Rubbish!' one shouted.

The other looked at us with open contempt. 'Strip,' he ordered. 'We're going to search you.'

My colleagues immediately obliged as they were absolutely in fear of the police, and soon three fully grown men were standing, cowed and as naked as the day they were born.

I was offended and fearful but I refused to be humiliated in this way. I stood, silent and unmoving, as my colleagues undressed.

My boss looked at me, his lip curling. 'You. I should have known. You took it.'

'I didn't steal your money,' I insisted.

'If you're innocent, why won't you strip?' one of the detectives asked.

Trapped, I stripped reluctantly down to my underpants, which I refused to remove.

The detectives shook out our clothes and then threw them back at us, instructing us to get dressed. Then they marched us outside to the police van, where we were violently shoved into the back. We were all terrified.

At the police station we were taken to an interrogation room and questioned, one by one, for hours. I was finally released late in the afternoon, just in time to get to my bus.

I didn't want to return to work the next morning but I needed the job so I went back. Besides, I was innocent.

I wasn't fired that day, or the next, or any time during the next four months, which took us to the end of the year, when I resigned. Nothing further was ever said about the missing money or the investigation but the imbalance of power was evident to all of us in that momentary but very real possibility that our lives were going to be destroyed by what was clearly a false accusation.

◆

In 1969, at the age of 19, I left Johannesburg to go and study towards a bachelor of science (B.Sc) at the University of Western Cape, which had been established as a college of the University of South Africa (Unisa) for people classified as coloured. The university offered limited training for lower to middle-level positions in schools, the civil service and other institutions designed to serve a separated coloured community.

At the end of the first semester, around the Easter holidays, I got a telegram from home. When I read it I almost fainted. My head was spinning and I felt dizzy. My little brother Desmond, just 9 years old, had died in a traffic accident.

I spent the next few days in a daze. I felt that I was in a bad dream and that I would wake up at some point. I took the train back to Johannesburg, a seemingly endless journey that actually lasted a night and a day.

Desmond had been killed by a truck right in front of our house, where he'd been playing with his friends – where I'd played all the time when I was younger. The driver was arrested and charged with culpable homicide. A few months later I was in the courtroom when the case was being heard. The driver was acquitted – he claimed it was Desmond's fault, because he and his friends had hopped onto the back of the truck to hitch a ride without the driver's knowledge, and Desmond had lost his footing and fallen under the vehicle. I knew this was simply not true – my brother was quiet and reserved, and would never have taken a risk like that.

This accident, which was almost unbearable for me, along with the routine violence we lived with in the townships, created a huge sense of vulnerability within me. Looking ahead, it seemed highly unlikely to me that I would live to see my 21st birthday.

And Desmond's death wasn't the last tragedy our family had to endure. Twenty years later, in 1989, when my brother Ephraim was 36 years old, he was killed by a gang in Riverlea, where he still lived in our family home.

In the wee hours of one morning, he and a friend were on their way home after an evening out. As they were crossing the railway line, they were confronted by a gang. Ephraim's friend managed to get away during the fight that ensued. Ephraim, however, was physically strong and fearless; he always held his ground in any fight and would never back off.

Later that day, the friend came around to the house to check on Ephraim, only to discover that he'd never made it home. Everyone went looking for him, and the police later informed us that a man had been killed on the railway crossing and was in the government mortuary.

My mother, Aunt Minnie and I went to the mortuary in Braamfontein, hoping and praying that by some miracle the dead man wasn't Ephraim. My mother and my aunt were too traumatised to go into the mortuary and it was left to me to perform the daunting task of identifying the body. When I saw my brother's corpse lying on the table I was devastated. He had severe injuries to his face and body, and I couldn't imagine how anyone could do something like this to another person. The cruelty was hard to fathom.

Ephraim didn't deserve a death like that. He'd had a tough upbringing: a father who'd deserted him at a young age, a school dropout by the age of 15, and imprisoned before the age of 20 for reasons I can't recall. He'd had no steady job for most of his life.

Following Ephraim's death, my mother and I raised his three daughters, together with their mum, Serena, who has since passed on. Today, Michelle and Angrenaide are both married, with children. Lesley Anne is single and lives with my mum. All of them live in Riverlea.

My brother Ephraim's murder was never investigated. It wasn't unusual for murders and crimes in general to go uninvestigated in those days: racism was clearly a factor but the police's lack of resources also played a part.

5

MOVING UP

As an adult, I desired not only more freedom but more space – life in our overcrowded Riverlea house was never comfortable. When I was growing up, I'd developed a close relationship with 'Aunt Emily', the mother of my close friend Willie Thompson – her surname was Lang but Willie had taken his father's surname – and in my late teens I moved into her less crowded home.

I met Amy, the woman who was to become my wife, when I was 20. Although my life was tough, I think Amy's was much tougher. Her stepfather, Fred Lotz, who married her mother, Francis (the same name as my mother but with a different spelling), was particularly mean to her when she was growing up. By the time I met her, Uncle Fred had mellowed, and in some ways seemed to be trying to atone for his past bad behaviour.

Amy fell pregnant and our daughter Althea was born in April of the following year. As soon as I laid my eyes on my newborn baby, very powerful paternal instincts were triggered, and I knew that I had to get married and take proper care of my young family. The idea that my daughter might grow up in a single-parent family, as had been the case with me, was simply unacceptable.

A few months later, soon after my 21st birthday, Amy and I were married in the magistrate's court. My friend from school, Clive Fortuin, and another schoolmate, Andrew Dippenaar, attended, and we had a lunch for close friends and family afterwards.

As a newly married couple, Amy and I had no accommodation of our own – I was staying with Aunt Emily, and Amy was with her parents in Noordgesig, a neighbouring township – so we continued living apart for several months. It was only towards the end of that year, 1971, that I managed to secure a flat in Riverlea, and moved in my young family. In 1973 I bought my first car, a secondhand Hillman Hunter on hire-purchase.

Our daughter Cheryl was born a year later, and our son Alvin was born in 1987 when I was 37.

◆

In 1974, when I was in my early 20s, the Johannesburg municipality ramped up the building of houses in Eldorado Park and I was able to rent a freestanding two-bedroomed house on a plot of about 400 square metres. Within a year, newly built freestanding houses in the area became available for purchase, and I quickly bought one. This was a significant step up for me, as it was the first time I was able to own property. It was a very emotional event.

We were very happy in the neighbourhood and got along well with all our neighbours. We all got to know each other and were supportive of one another. For example, the ambulance service was very unreliable and I had to rush sick people to hospital on a number of occasions. I also tutored some of the neighbourhood children in mathematics and science.

There were some challenges. My daughters attended school at St Barnabas in Bosmont, and we had to arrange private transport for them, as public transport wasn't available. I was serving articles in central Johannesburg at the time and travelling to and from work in heavy traffic daily was a nightmare.

During the apartheid era, black citizens didn't have the luxury of buying houses close to amenities and schools because their options were substantially reduced. White citizens are generally unable to relate to the pain and suffering that this denial caused, simply because they've never been denied basic rights in this country. When black citizens fight for their rights, white citizens often wonder what the fuss is all about.

An American visitor to Soweto in the mid-1980s, Linda Saulsby, described life in the townships as it applied to those around Soweto too, including Riverlea. She noticed a small, middle-class area, and noted that the people who lived there were 'the front guard of those who had clawed their way out of Soweto's lowlands. They all had relatives and friends who were still trapped there. They worried about falling back. They feared the capricious action of white policemen that could befall them on any day.' She went on to describe 'the millions [who] lived in the vast lowlands in the squalor of tin shacks, uncollected garbage, oppressive pollution, and untreated disease, on arid land. A large number of blacks commuted several hours each day to service jobs in Johannesburg and its surrounding communities; most of the women who worked as domestics in white households came home to Soweto only on weekends.'

◆

In 1970 I registered – helped in this process by my ex high-school commerce teacher and mentor, Brian Theron – for a B.Com at Unisa, the distance-learning institution. I threw myself into these studies, devoting six years to completing the degree on a part-time basis. It was transformative, paving the way for me to pursue a career as a chartered accountant.

My time at Unisa was also important for the strong friendships I established with some of my fellow students. Cassim Gassiep and Leonard Phillips[9] were both also studying to become chartered accountants and we formed a very tight study group. We would get together to do our assignments and write mock examinations, then mark each other's scripts. I found this approach invaluable.

Another good friend was Hadley Simons, a brilliant mathematician who was studying to become a scientist. Sadly, Hadley had limited career opportunities in the field and couldn't fulfil his ambitions.[10]

There was another reason why that first year of study stands out so starkly for me to this day: it was the year I discovered James Arthur Baldwin, an African-American novelist, playwright, essayist, poet and activist. One of his books, *The Fire Next Time*, was prescribed for my English course. In one of the essays, Baldwin warned that

---

[9] Both Cassim and Leonard qualified. Leonard couldn't deal with the apartheid constraints and emigrated to Canada. Cassim has since passed away.

[10] Hadley died in a car accident at the age of 39. I remain in contact with his wife Shirley, his daughter Gillian and his grandchild Chandre, who is taking after her grandfather – she's doing exceptionally well at university and hopes to pursue a career in law.

if white America didn't change its attitudes and policies towards African Americans and alter the conditions under which they were forced to live, violence would result. This warning was prophetic, and we've all seen the evidence of this over the last few years and witnessed the continuing challenges African Americans still endure. Civil-rights movements such as Black Lives Matter remain engaged in a fierce struggle for equality, fairness and justice, despite the passage of progressive legislation and the election of Barack Obama as US president for two terms.

Over the years since then I've read a number of Baldwin's books and essays, and as an activist myself, I take strength and inspiration from his speeches and writings. Baldwin took part in a fascinating debate at Cambridge University in 1965. The subject of the debate was 'Has the American Dream been achieved at the expense of the American Negro?' and he was invited to speak in favour of the motion, while William F Buckley, the editor of right-wing newspaper, spoke against it. Baldwin won the debate fair and square.

As I absorbed Baldwin articulating the plight of the African-Americans, it resonated powerfully with me as a black person growing up in apartheid South Africa. But in South Africa we have one critical advantage not available to African Americans, and that's that we're by far in the majority. At the time of the Baldwin debate, African Americans represented one ninth of the population; according to the 2019 estimate, that number has since risen to 13.4 percent. In South Africa, however, it's whites who represent a mere nine percent of the population.

It is true that since colonial times, the wealth in this country has been built at the expense of black people. Even today, 27 years since the advent of our new democracy, this wealth remains concentrated in the hands of our white compatriots. In a country where black folk are by far in the majority, you don't have to be a genius to see that this level of poverty and inequality is simply not sustainable.

Our challenge is to find a radical way to bridge the wealth gap and reduce poverty. We simply don't have the luxury of time for incremental change over the next hundred years. Baldwin's warning rings loud and clear: we face the stark choice of radical change or unprecedented violence.

◆

When I first registered for my degree, I knew little about the accounting profession, but I did know that I had to complete articles of clerkship and also write the notoriously difficult board exam. And the accounting profession in the mid-1970s was lily-white: it was very difficult for a 'non-white' to get articles; for black aspirant accountants there were huge barriers put in the way.

Not many accounting firms, including the major international firms, were prepared to employ African, Indian or coloured people as articled clerks for a number of reasons, including racial prejudice and client resistance. At that stage, a few of my Indian friends in my study group were serving their articles, but others had tried and failed numerous times to secure articles.

Undeterred, I selected three firms at random from the vacancies advertised in the monthly *Accountancy Journal*. The *Accountancy Journal*, published by the South African Institute of Chartered Accountants (SAICA), was recommended reading in my Unisa courses. I'd tried to get hold of it by going from bookstore to bookstore, without any success. Eventually I was told that I should go to the SAICA offices to obtain a copy. I did so and found it so informative that I subscribed to it. I became increasingly aware of the profession by becoming an avid reader of the journal.

I wrote to the three companies whose details I'd found in the journal, giving details of my progress at university and mentioning my race so that they weren't fooled by my Afrikaans surname, and then subsequently forced to pretend to me that the vacancy for which I'd applied had already been filled when they finally met me face to face and realised I wasn't white.

Unknown to me at the time, but working enormously in my favour, was the fact that the profession had recently adopted a voluntary code of employment in terms of which they'd made a commitment to hire black clerks. Within days I was invited for an interview by Schwartz Fine in Johannesburg.

There was no doubt that I was now at a significant fork in the road, a defining moment. Articles would change the trajectory of my life in a way that was hard to fathom. Failure was simply not an option.

I had a restless night before the day of the interview and got up much earlier than usual the next morning. I took extra care with my grooming. I set off early as I couldn't risk being late. On my way to

Schwartz Fine, I stopped at a restaurant to grab some coffee from the takeaway counter around the side – black folk weren't allowed in restaurants.

I got to the reception with 10 minutes to spare.

'Good morning,' the receptionist said, a little frostily. 'Can I help you?'

'I'm here for an interview as an articled clerk,' I told her.

She frowned, then laughed, seeming incredulous. Then she shrugged and made a call. When she looked at me again, her expression had changed – she was blushing. 'Someone will come and fetch you shortly,' she said. 'Have a seat.'

A smartly dressed young woman came and ushered me through to the spacious office of Arnold Kane, with whom I was meeting. David Lopatie, another of the partners, was there with him. Unlike the receptionist, their demeanour was warm and friendly. There was some small talk to put me at ease. I was encouraged and felt relaxed.

I sensed that they had already decided to hire me on the strength of my academic credentials, which made my work ethic and discipline self-evident: you don't get that far as a Unisa student without those qualities. But they wanted to get a sense of who I was as a person – in other words, my family, character and values.

It helped that they were transparent and candid: this was a new experience for them too, Kane explained; they had never employed a black person as an articled clerk before and they didn't know if I would be able to fit into what was a white-dominant culture.

All three of us were realistic. We knew there would be challenges.

But they were prepared to employ me and I was determined to make it work.

My employment offer was subject to two strict conditions. First, I would not go out to clients who, in their view, were not ready for a black person to have access to their accounting records. Instead, I would work within the office's bookkeeping division, where there was limited client contact. I was promised that a transfer to 'external audit' would be considered once the social climate had changed, but there was a real possibility of my serving out my entire contract working within the internal bookkeeping division. Second, they advised that I would not have any long-term career prospects within the firm: once my contract had expired, they would expect me to go and work in my own community.

I wasn't keen on these strict conditions but theirs was likely to be the only offer on the table, so I informed them a few days later that they were acceptable to me. That said, as I reflect on that interview today, I now understand their dilemma. The apartheid laws were very strictly policed and enforced by the government, and while the firm was trying to be progressive, they obviously had to protect their business interests. Also, as they had no experience of working with black professionals, they had to manage the situation very carefully.

6

A BRAND NEW WORLD

My entry into the accounting profession in January 1975 was a truly life-changing event in at least two respects. First, I had no doubt in my ability to complete my studies and obtain the much sought-after qualification of chartered accountant, and I sensed that the qualification would open doors of opportunity that before had been closed to me simply on the basis of the colour of my skin.

Second, this was the first time since I'd left school that I was looked at as a full human being rather than as subhuman. The release of oppression I felt in my body and soul is hard to describe. The opportunity to compete with other aspirant accountants on an equal basis, regardless of race, gender or religion, was inspiring and exhilarating.

My destiny was now in my own hands. It was entirely up to me to seize the opportunity and do whatever was necessary to achieve the objective. No sacrifice would be too great, no effort would be spared and no excuses would be made.

On 16 June 1976, 18 months into my employment, a series of demonstrations and protests began in Soweto, led by black school-children who objected to being forced to learn in Afrikaans. Because I was black, most of my white colleagues assumed that I understood what was happening and asked me to explain. They appeared to be genuinely perplexed – and disapproving. Why were the students protesting, they asked. What was wrong with Afrikaans as a medium of instruction? Was it worthwhile risking lives? What were the students trying to achieve?

I was frustrated and perplexed by the almost complete lack of empathy and understanding of the student resistance to Afrikaans as a symbol of apartheid. My colleagues knew, after all, that apartheid, formally introduced when the Nationalist Party came to power in 1948, was maintained through the violence of the army and police; that black people were denied the vote; that black people were treated as second-class citizens; that black political organisations were banned and political leaders imprisoned; that, in 1973, the United Nations had defined apartheid as a 'crime against humanity'; and that black people were engaged in a struggle for freedom that had lasted generations.

I tried to explain as best I could that the conflict had arisen when the apartheid state had decreed the use of Afrikaans ('the language of the oppressor', as Bishop Desmond Tutu later put it) in black schools as a medium of instruction, along with English, while white, coloured and Indian schools were free to choose their language of instruction.

In a sense I was conflicted. In my particular case, my home language was Afrikaans, the language spoken by most coloured people, and Afrikaans had been the language of instruction in all my subjects throughout my schooling. I'd switched to English when I started studying at university in 1969 but the reason for my switch hadn't been political. I reasoned that English was a global language and was most commonly used in commerce and industry, and I felt that being proficient in English would be beneficial to my career.

Notwithstanding my personal circumstances, I had a very clear understanding of why the students were protesting and I was empathetic. I felt the protests were justified. Personally, however, my main priority at the time was to complete my articles and qualify as a chartered accountant. I had no doubt whatsoever that at some point in the future I would become involved in the struggle for freedom in one way or another.

Tragically, it's estimated that over the three days of student protests, there were up to 700 deaths and 4 000 injuries.

◆

Bernard Fridman was another articled clerk – a white one – at Schwartz Fine at the time, and he and I became good friends. He was temporarily working a six-hour day, as he needed the late afternoons to train for the Comrades Marathon, a very popular ultramarathon that takes place annually between Durban and Pietermaritzburg. Bernie's office was on the fifteenth floor of the Schwartz Fine highrise building overlooking the Supreme Law Courts, and my office was across the corridor from him.

'Jeff was very friendly,' Bernie recalls, 'although during those first few months he found the environment tough to navigate. During my short working life up until then I had predominantly been surrounded by white colleagues. Jeff and I bonded as mates, and for me it was fantastic having this friendship. He told me about the life experiences of a young man of colour in apartheid South Africa. As our friendship developed, so our conversations became more serious and intellectual. We spent many hours discussing, debating and deliberating the ills of apartheid and dreaming of a free and democratic South Africa.'

Bernie's friendship meant so much to me. He was my sounding board, and he helped me to deal with the environment and acclimatise.

Bernie continues, 'My lunches with Jeff were the highlights of my day. At that time, people of colour weren't permitted to attend regular restaurants, which were reserved for whites only. More or less at that time, however, the government passed a law allowing people of colour to attend restaurants that were frequented by international tourists. The Wimpy restaurant on the top floor of the Carlton Centre was thus classified a "non-apartheid" area. This became our lunch hideout, a place we cherished as one in which to socialise outside of our office environment.

'Under extreme international pressure later that year, the government extended the "international restaurant" law to include restaurants in five-star hotels. A lunch that stands out in my mind is the day after this law was relaxed, when Jeff and I were walking past the Carlton Hotel on our way to the Wimpy, and I said to him, "Come on, let's go in here, to the Carlton Hotel Koffiehuis." It was one of my favourite lunchtime spots. I didn't wait for an answer, I just walked into the hotel lobby and headed towards the Koffiehuis. I look back and saw a bewildered Jeff, reluctant to follow. I encouraged him to follow me into the restaurant.'

Walking into the Koffiehuis that day was a big deal for me. I worried that the white patrons would think I was about to start swinging from the curtains!

Bernie continues, 'Then another obstacle had to be overcome: there was a long line of white people waiting to be seated. I noticed the bar area was free and suggested we walk in and ignore the line. I felt the tension and a very strange atmosphere as Jeff and I walked towards the bar area, passing all the whites standing in line waiting to be seated. As we sat down at the bar, Jeff said this was possibly one of the most stressful moments he had ever experienced.

'Next, we had to order food. In my naivety I was unaware that Jeff hadn't frequented an upmarket restaurant before and this was possibly his "breaking of the glass ceiling". I had to talk him through the menu.'

Bear in mind that I didn't even taste pizza until I was 24 years old!

Bernie continues, 'We decided to have my favourite dish, the Dutch Dip, which was a sliced beef filling in a long fresh baguette, with gravy on the side in a small bowl. When our order arrived, I asked Jeff to please excuse me using my fingers. He awkwardly used his cutlery to cut up his roll but after a few bites he admitted that it was difficult to try to eat that way – but he added that eating it with his hands would lead to inevitable accusations that he was a k… and didn't know how to use a knife and fork.

'His remark saddened me be beyond words, that something I took so for granted could have been so humiliating for my good buddy. All of this was because of an evil and humiliating political and social policy. I've never forgotten that moment and sadly I still think about it when I think of South Africa and the part I played in that destructive policy.'

I've always been grateful to Bernie for being so brave that day, and allowing me to have that experience. We went back to the restaurant a number of times after that, and the Dutch Dip became my favourite.

Bernie was also with me when we both got our university results. I drove with him to Pretoria, where the results were posted on a Unisa noticeboard. We'd both passed all our exams, which meant we could both graduate.

Bernie remembers, 'I couldn't wait to get home to tell my dad that I'd passed. Jeff looked sad and I asked him what was wrong. He said, "Bernie, I don't have anyone close to me to tell that I've passed. My family just don't understand what I've achieved."'

I was perceived by family and friends to be studying bookkeeping. There were young women in the community who'd dropped out of school – who had never even completed matric – and they were working as bookkeepers. Trying to explain the difference to my family was impossible.

Bernie recalls, 'My heart went out to Jeff as I realised how lucky and privileged I was in having the support and understanding of a family that encouraged me to study and get educated. Jeff seemed so alone, as he bravely took on the world in his pursuit for higher education and basic human equality.

'In the car driving back to Johannesburg I said to Jeff, "I'm just one of thousands of white students about to graduate, not really anything to shout about. You, however, are unique, and this degree is a stepping stone for you, building towards an incredible financial future that you will one day cherish."'

There was another upsetting aspect to this. As a coloured person, I wasn't permitted to go to the graduation ceremony at the main campus in Pretoria; I was told to go to the graduation ceremony for coloured graduates in Athlone, Cape Town – most of South Africa's coloured population lived in the Western Cape. In protest, I refused. Four years later, by the time I graduated with my B.Compt (bachelor of accounting science) (hons) in 1980, there was one graduation ceremony reserved exclusively for whites, coloureds and Indians, and another separate ceremony for Africans. That time, I swallowed my pride and attended.

◆

I completed my articles in 1979. Around the same time, Schwartz Fine merged with Arthur Andersen, one of the major global accounting firms at the time.

I remained with Arthur Anderson until 1981, when I wanted to join the Industrial Development Corporation, a state-owned enterprise, in order to get much-sought-after commercial experience. But the Industrial Development Corporation informed me that they didn't employ black professionals, so instead I joined Alex Aiken and Carter (which subsequently became KPMG) as an audit manager.

I really enjoyed working for the firm. I was trusted and respected by many of my colleagues, and a partnership in the near future seemed attainable.

Towards the end of my two-year stint, there was a crisis with one of our clients, a subsidiary of a US company. The audit manager, whom I shall call John Smith (not his real name), had apparently fallen out with the CEO for reasons that remain unclear to me, and the CEO was so incensed that he insisted that the firm should replace John with immediate effect.

I was appointed as John's replacement. I was confident that with hard work and long hours, the job could be done satisfactorily, and I put in the effort and time to complete it within the required deadlines. The American parent company was a signatory to the Sullivan Principles, developed in 1977 to apply economic pressure on South Africa in protest of apartheid, and consisting of seven requirements a company was to demand for its employees as a condition for doing business, including the equal treatment of employees regardless of their race, both within and outside of the workplace.

At the end of the audit, as a token of appreciation, I was offered a scholarship by the company to study part-time for an MBA at a South African university. I declined the offer because I felt that my chartered accountant qualification was more than adequate, given my aspiration to become a partner in my firm.

A few months later, a number of senior positions within the firm became available, two levels away from partnership. I felt that I was

one of the obvious choices but on the day before the announce-
ments, I was informed that I wouldn't be one of the candidates. The
reason, I was told, was because of resistance to a man of colour by a
group of very influential partners – apparently they required more
time to deal with their own prejudices and bigotry.

My boss suggested I consider a move to one of the company's
branches in the then 'bantustan' homelands, where I would stand a
far better chance of promotion. I had two options: to stay and hope
that attitudes would change, or to leave. But the fact of the matter
was that I had an overpowering instinct that I did not belong in
such a firm. 'Given the circumstances you've just outlined, you can't
expect me to hang around here,' I told my boss.

He was taken aback and asked me to go home and think about it
before making any decision.

I was absolutely gutted, but the worst was yet to come. The next
day, the list of names of the candidates was posted on the noticeboard. John Smith's was among them.[11] I immediately tendered my
resignation. I was seething at the treatment I'd received after giving
my all and showing what I could do. It convinced me that blacks
weren't welcome in any of the mainstream firms, and there would
be no point for me to leave one and join another.

What inspired and motivated me to get through the tough times?
As past American first lady Eleanor Roosevelt said, 'You learn by

---

[11] I learned many years later that John Smith was eventually appointed as a partner. He then left
the firm to join a family business, and not long afterwards was convicted and jailed for fraud.

living – you gain strength, courage and confidence by every experience in which you really stop to look fear in the face. You are able
to say to yourself, "I lived through this horror. I can take the next
thing that comes along."' Always remember that you don't know
how strong you are until being strong is the only option that you
have.

And with the benefit of hindsight I now see that maybe the
harsh treatment I endured was exactly what I needed at the time
– it spurred me both to set up my own practice, and to launch
the Association of Black Accountants of South Africa. That anger
fresh in my mind provided the stimulus to lead the launch of an
organisation that was to challenge the mainstream firms, with the
ultimate objective of eliminating the continued marginalisation of
and denial of opportunities to black accountants.

7

INTO BUSINESS

In 1983, I joined Lack Flaum and Associates, a two-partner firm. I'd worked with Wolfie Lack during my tenure at Schwartz Fine, and within a year I was offered a partnership, which was exceptionally progressive given the racial climate at the time. But I'd already decided to go into private practice because of a strong desire to have more control over my career advancement. I didn't realise, however, until that moment in 1985, just how shackled black business was by apartheid.

At the time, most auditing and accounting practices operated from Johannesburg's central business district, so naturally, that's where I needed to establish my office. I contacted a number of estate agents to inquire about vacant office premises. There was a lot of space available and I promptly arranged appointments to view some of the premises.

My reception at the estate agents' offices was depressingly uniform. The receptionist would ask me, usually rudely, what I wanted. I would explain that I was there by appointment, to view office premises. The receptionist would look surprised or puzzled or angry or amused, and disappear into a back office for a few moments, before reappearing to tell me that there were no vacant premises at that time.

This was very frustrating and exasperating, and I decided to tell them upfront when I called that I was a black man seeking to establish an accounting practice – this at least would save time and embarrassment.

Eventually I connected with an estate agent who was very helpful and explained that in order to be able to rent premises, I needed to apply for a permit from the Department of Community Development. This was because the notorious Group Areas Act specified that if a black person wished to work for themselves, they could only do so in the townships – unless an exception was granted, by way of a permit, by the relevant authority. So I applied for the permit and on that basis I was allowed to rent offices.

Securing premises wasn't my only hurdle. Obtaining a loan from a bank, any bank, to fund working capital, proved to be much more difficult. I walked the streets of central Johannesburg all day, visiting all the banks in town, to try to secure a loan, but to no avail. I was a black man, and the stereotype was that we didn't repay loans. The fact that I was a chartered accountant didn't come into it. It didn't help that I had no collateral to provide, nor anyone with a strong enough personal balance sheet to act as surety.

Just as I was about to give up, I was invited to a dinner at the house of Freda van Rooyen (no relation), one of my white friends. There I met Dr Jurgen Smith, who happened to be the deputy chief executive officer of the Small Business Development Corporation (SBDC), a partnership between government and the private sector to help fund small businesses. I appealed to Jurgen for much-needed help.

The SBDC provided a guarantee and I was able to secure a

loan from a bank.[12] I went about putting money into my business, acquiring clients and doing my work, and six months later, I had a promising practice going.

Then one morning I had a surprise visit from two white inspectors from the Department of Community Development.

It didn't start well.

'What are you doing here, in these offices?' the one man asked.

'I'm running an accounting practice,' I said, reasonably.

'Your permit hasn't been granted yet,' the second man snapped. 'You're not allowed to be here. You've been working here illegally for six months.'

My heart sank. 'The estate agent who rented me these offices told me this was common practice – that as long as the permit had been applied for, I could move in.'

'Well, he was wrong,' the first man said. He'd taken out a clipboard and was making notes on it.

This was really bad news. One of my first clients, Aubrey Khanyile, a lawyer based in Krugersdorp to the west of Johannesburg, had had the same problem as I had securing premises. His permit application had been turned down, and Aubrey who, like me, had already moved into his offices, was told to move out. He refused to vacate the premises and became embroiled in a tough legal tussle with the municipality.

I decided to appeal to the men's rational side. 'I heard it can take

[12] I repaid the loan in full. A few years later I was appointed as a non-executive director of the SBDC and worked very closely with Jurgen, and our relationship endured long after we both left the SBDC.

up to a year for the permit to be granted,' I said. 'I'm sure you can understand, sir, that I couldn't afford to sit at home doing nothing while I waited.'

'That's neither here nor there,' he said, still making notes. 'Where do you live?'

'In Eldorado Park,' I answered.

'So what's wrong with running your accounting practice there?'

'Well, my clients come from all over, not just Eldorado Park,' I explained. 'The Joburg city centre is the most accessible place to be for all of them.'

The second man raised his eyebrows as if in disbelief. 'We'll get back to you,' he said, ominously, as the two of them left.

I had some sleepless nights for the next few weeks – not only would I be in big trouble if my permit application wasn't approved, but I lacked the working capital to start all over again somewhere else. To my great relief, however, I finally got a phonecall to say that my application had been approved.

While my main office was in central Johannesburg, the number of clients I had from Eldorado Park necessitated establishing a satellite office in the local shopping centre. In 1990, when I merged my practice with Deloitte, I transferred that satellite office, including the clients, to Lloyd Theunissen, a good friend. Lloyd ran the practice successfully for a number of years.[13]

---

[13] In later years Lloyd continued to run the accounting practice but from his home office in Mulbarton. He passed away in 2022 and the practice is now run by his daughter, Amore Watkins.

65

Most of my clients were black business people or professionals, including lawyers. I have fond memories of many of them, such as Vincent Moffat, who owned a number of wholesale and retail businesses and today still operates businesses in the township although he lives in the upmarket suburb of Bushkoppies on the border of Eldorado Park.

But my eyes were also opened to the dark side of business, when one of my clients put enormous pressure on me to manipulate his financial statements. He explained that he'd applied for a loan from the bank and that unless the financial statements reflected a healthy profit, the loan wouldn't be approved. I resisted the pressure and sought advice from the South African Institute of Chartered Accountants (SAICA). I signed off on the financials with no changes, and resigned from the audit.

In another case, a potential client brought me a set of draft financial statements, prepared by a major auditing firm, which reflected a healthy profit and significant tax exposure as a result. He asked me if there was anything I could do to reduce the tax exposure – for a healthy fee. I told him politely that if he couldn't get what he wanted from his auditors, who had all the necessary technical expertise available, there was nothing I could do. That was the last I saw of him.

These early experiences left an indelible mark on me. As auditors, we have to conduct ourselves with the utmost integrity, regardless of the consequences. We may lose clients and fees in some cases but we must never lose sight of our primary purpose, which is to give assurance to third parties that they may rely on the fairness of the financial statements in making financial decisions.

◆

My client base also included trade unions for black workers. In the main, I worked with the National Council of Trade Unions (Nactu) and their affiliates. I wasn't only responsible for their accounting and auditing, but also assisted them in their wage negotiations with employers. These negotiations were understandably difficult, as workers were poorly protected and employers were more concerned about maximising shareholder returns than paying workers fairly.

Once I worked on a difficult case with one of the union organisers, a young man by the name of Lele. Within months of concluding the matter he was killed in a drive-by shooting. We had worked well together; I admired his dedication and commitment to his job, and I was devastated. We were never able to establish the motive for the assassination.

I became an expert at understanding the business landscape. I understood that none of the Johannesburg Stock Exchange (JSE) listed companies were run by black people, and only a handful even had a black person on their board. As a result of the various discriminatory laws in the country, black businesses were generally confined to the townships, and, as I had experienced myself, access to capital to grow their businesses was almost nonexistent.

◆

My political education only really started in the mid-1980s, when I was in my mid-30s, and in particular during my involvement with the Association for the Advancement of Black Accountants (Abasa) (which I discuss more fully in chapter 9).

I had almost no political awareness growing up. When the Sharpeville massacre happened in March 1960, I'd just celebrated my 10th birthday, and during the Rivonia trial of 1963-1964 I was in my early teenage years.[14] So although I recall the reaction and the anger in the township, I was too young to understand fully or be involved.

Politics was never discussed in my home. We were poor and too preoccupied with surviving. Politics was also never discussed at school, even at high school, because it was strictly forbidden by the Department of Education and most teachers feared that they would jeopardise their jobs and their career prospects if they ventured into that forbidden territory. History was one of my high-school subjects but we were taught absolutely nothing about the political struggle or the liberation movement.

Some of my friends became politically aware and active when they got to university. I spent only one semester physically on a university campus, at the University of the Western Cape, which was

---

[14] On 21 March 1960, after a day of demonstrations against the hated pass laws, a crowd of about 7 000 protesters went to the police station in Sharpeville. The police opened fire on them, killing 69 people and injuring 180 others. Many were shot in the back as they fled. The defendants in the so-called Rivonia Trial a few years later were 12 members of the ANC, including Nelson Mandela, who were accused under the 1962 Sabotage Act with attempting to violently overthrow the South African government. They were sentenced to life imprisonment.

hardly enough time to be exposed to politics. After that I studied by correspondence through Unisa, where there was naturally limited contact with other students. It didn't help that political literature associated with black political leaders and the liberation movement was banned.

When I was in my 30s and began travelling abroad, I would trawl bookshops in foreign countries for literature on the South African liberation movements. I was so captivated that I would often read until the early hours of the morning. Because the literature was banned, I would leave it in the hotel when I left.

The Black Lawyers Association (BLA) legal education centre was one of my clients during the tenure of the prominent lawyer Godfrey Pitje, who'd served his articles at Nelson Mandela and Oliver Tambo's law firm – the first attorney firm in the country run by black partners – in the 1950s. I had long and deep political conversations with Godfrey and regarded him as one of my political mentors.

Another was Dikgang Moseneke, a director of the education centre at the time, and who was a frequent guest speaker at Abasa annual conventions. Dikgang, who belonged to the Pan Africanist Congress (PAC), surprisingly pointed me in the direction of the African National Congress (ANC). In a recent discussion with him, he told me that it took only about 10 minutes for him to realise that I was a charterist, meaning someone who aligns himself with the Freedom Charter, the 1955 statement of core principles of the South African Congress Alliance, which included the ANC and its allies.

❖

PART 3

BUILDING A LEGACY

'Someone's sitting in the shade today because someone
planted a tree a long time ago.'

Warren Buffett

8

THE BIG LEAGUES

In 1988, I attended a seminar hosted by SAICA on how to facilitate the entry of black folk into the profession. Among the speakers was Tim Store, a partner at international financial services firm Deloitte and an early supporter of Abasa, and a professor from one of the white universities who considered himself an expert on the topic.

Tim's presentation was very progressive and advocated strongly for the profession to facilitate access for black people by, among other things, supporting bridging programmes at universities to compensate for the poor quality of education in black schools.

The professor's presentation, by contrast, took a racist slant – blacks were simply not cut out for the profession for a host of reasons, he said, including their lack of business culture and conceptual thinking which, in his opinion, were prerequisites for entry into the profession. Furthermore, an enormous amount of resources would be required if bridging programmes were to be successful.

I was the only black person in the room, and I was sitting right at the back so he couldn't see me.

Not unexpectedly, I took strong exception to his remarks and raised my hand. When he acknowledged me, I said, 'Professor, as you can see, I am a black man. I don't have a business background but I'm a qualified chartered accountant. I studied by way of correspondence with Unisa and I never participated in any bridging programme specifically designed for black people.'

The man was visibly startled and it took him a while to regain his composure. When he did, all he could bluster was, 'You're an exception.' This was the typical response I got whenever I challenged racial stereotypes.

During the refreshment break, a man came up to me and introduced himself as Tim Curtis, the managing partner of Deloitte. Tim said that he'd been impressed with my intervention. He gave me his business card and asked me to contact him so that we could continue the conversation.

As I reflect today on that seminar and the naked racism of the professor, I realise that he'd unintentionally given me a platform which, in turn, led to my being noticed by Tim and that, in turn, led to a significant change in my career trajectory.

◆

In another life-changing move, I entered into a joint venture with Deloitte in 1988. In terms of this agreement, Deloitte seconded staff to me. I had an ever-increasing workload and was grateful for the help.

Over the next two years, I got to know most of Deloitte's approximately 100 partners. I attended both annual partner meetings, which dealt with a review of past performance, strategy and focus for the ensuing year. I also worked with a number of partners on various client matters.

On 2 February 1990, just a few days before my 40th birthday, then state president FW de Klerk gave a historic speech in parliament, announcing the unbanning of the ANC, the PAC and the South African Communist Party. Listening to it was almost surreal; it felt like I was having an out-of-body experience. For the first time in my life I could sense political freedom wasn't only possible within my lifetime, but that it was imminent.

The statement released by the United Democratic Front (UDF) on the same day was cautious yet hopeful, validating my own view that freedom was in sight. They also reached out to white people in an effort to calm their fears that black people would seek revenge when the tables were turned. The UDF spoke of a commitment to a non-racial democratic state, which strongly resonated with me.

This new sense of freedom was a game changer for me. Up to that point in my life, my dream had been to build the largest black accounting practice in the country. I suddenly saw the possibility of merging my business with Deloitte in the hope of being part of building a non-racial practice.

The management of Deloitte was truly visionary and progressive, and we shared that dream. And, indeed, Deloitte immediately decided to embark on an active programme to diversify their client base to include more of the black-owned businesses in the country. This was primarily my client base, so Deloitte initiated a discussion around a potential take-over of my firm, a move that made a lot of sense to me.

A complicating factor was that, simultaneously, Deloitte was pursuing merger discussions with Pim Goldby, a firm roughly equal in size to Deloitte. Tim Curtis, the senior partner of Deloitte, was very keen to bring me into the merged Deloitte Pim Goldby firm as a partner. I was, after all, also better positioned than anyone else to help the firm navigate a rapidly changing political landscape. The problem was that I didn't know the Pim Goldby partners and vice versa.

Tim arranged for me to have a discussion with Bev Humphris, one of the senior partners of Pim Goldby. Bev and I met and explored why it would make sense for my practice to be absorbed by the newly merged firm; the onus was on me to persuade Bev that such a move would be mutually beneficial. I must have put my case convincingly, because Bev then arranged for me to meet with the executive committee of Pim Goldby, which comprised about fifteen of the firm's most senior partners.

On the day, Mike Rippon, a Deloitte partner with whom I had a strong relationship, accompanied me to provide moral support. There were no questions concerning my knowledge, skills and experience, but the ones they did ask were tough and covered my professional and family background, and my political views and affiliations. They asked me whether my support of the ANC could lead to political tension or polarisation. I said that I would never allow political differences to interfere with my duties and responsibilities, and that I would always behave responsibly and not cause any embarrassment to the firm or its clients.

Ironically, a few years later, the managing partner of the firm at the time, Martin Shaw, granted me permission to work with Tito

Mboweni, who'd been a very prominent member of the ANC in exile. As a consequence, many of the meetings and workshops of the ANC were held at the Deloitte offices in Woodmead and I was even able to provide refreshments at the firm's expense. Any visitor signing the attendance register at the security gate would have sworn that the ANC had offices in the complex!

Tito represented the ANC in the finance committee of the transitional government established by the ANC and the National Party, and was later appointed as Minister of Labour in the Mandela administration. Arising from my relationship with Tito, I was often invited to meetings between ANC and government representatives during the transition period, and that paved the way for me to be appointed as special advisor to Stella Sigcau, Minister of Public Enterprises in 1996-1997.

◆

When I became a partner in the newly formed Deloitte Pim Goldby by a unanimous vote in 1990, I thought that the circumstances had changed sufficiently for me to find a house closer to work. The Deloitte offices were in Woodmead, Sandton, so I started searching for a house in the area. The Group Areas Act was still in place and I discovered that estate agents were reluctant to take a risk, so my search proved fruitless.

Two years later I tried again, and this time the estate agents were a lot more helpful. I was informed that if I found a suitable house, however, given the colour of my skin, I would have to obtain written permission from my white neighbours in order to be able to purchase it. This condition didn't sit comfortably with me and I abandoned the search once again.

Finally, in 1993, I tried for a third time, and this time I was able to purchase a house in Fourways Gardens, Sandton, with no hassles at all. A predominantly white area planted with lots of trees, it's a gated area with 24-hour armed security. The suburb contains almost a thousand 'character homes' – basically, houses with unique features and personalities – on large stands.

It seemed as if we'd finally found a safe and pleasant place to live. However, no sooner had we moved in than the neighbour, realising we were a black family, started construction to raise the wall between our properties by more than two metres.

The high wall he planned would spoil our view, so I approached him about this. He was extremely hostile and stubbornly told me that he was going to erect the wall whether or not I agreed.

I lodged a complaint with the municipality and they forced him to restrict the height of the wall to below two metres. Not long afterwards, he sold his property and moved elsewhere. It was no great loss – the same neighbour had confronted my wife Amy, speaking down to her in a racist manner.

Amy hadn't been intimidated and had held her ground. Amy also hadn't hesitated to stand up for our son, Alvin, in similar circumstances. As the only person of colour at his exclusive school, Alvin had had an altercation with another boy, and Amy immediately went to chat with the teacher and encourage an investigation rather than allowing the teacher to simply take action against Alvin.

Our new and predominantly white neighbourhood was very different to what we were accustomed to. In the black neighbourhoods, we knew most of our neighbours by name and there was always friendly banter between us. We were also generally supportive of one another when the circumstances warranted it. My new neighbours, however, kept to themselves and I never got to know any of them except for one family who had a son, Justin, who was the same age as Alvin. The boys became friends, and through that friendship our families got to know each other and got along exceptionally well. Sadly, they moved out a few years later and we lost contact.

We also discovered that white people, certainly in my neighbourhood, tended to move house quite often. We still live in the same house to this day, and are probably one of the longest-tenured residents in the neighbourhood. I still don't know any of the surrounding families, who mainly keep to themselves. We've adjusted to this culture over the years and are now also happy to keep to ourselves.

◆

When I was appointed as a partner in Deloitte in 1990, the firm had four black partners and two female partners, representing two percent and one percent, respectively, of the overall partnership of about 200. Today, 43 percent of the partners are black and 36 percent are female, and my prediction is that within the next 10-15 years, black male and female partners will become the majority.

This means that whites will become a minority group and they have to start reflecting now on what the implications might be for them. I would hope that they wouldn't feel threatened by this inevitable change as they will still have a significant role to play in the profession and in the broader economy.

These reflections make me realise just how screwed up we were back then in South Africa. I realise now more than ever that all this is a sad part of our history, and white folks probably had little or no knowledge of how apartheid affected the daily lives of black people. While black folk had to leave the townships to go and work in the white areas, the opposite was true for white folk, who would never dare enter a township on their own; the whole culture was totally foreign to them.

◆

I worked for Deloitte for almost 10 years. During that time – and later in my career – I realised how vital it was for auditors to be scrupulously honest and behave with the utmost integrity.

Auditors play a significant role in business and in society in general. Investors, who are generally far removed from the operations of the companies in which they invest, rely very heavily on auditors to conduct an audit of the financial affairs of companies and express an audit opinion on the fairness of the financial information. The numbers are what they are, and the management has no business manipulating them or 'cooking the books'. In turn, the auditors have no business aiding and abetting management as and when they may wish to manipulate the numbers.

The consequences of false reporting are often disastrous for investors. Think of all the examples of fraudulent financial statements we've seen in recent years, such as in the cases of Steinhoff, VBS Mutual Bank and Tongaat Hulett.[15] Think of all the investors who made tremendous sacrifices over a lifetime to save for their retirement, and how tragic is it that these people, who put their faith in auditors, have had their life savings wiped out.

Sadly, these days accounting bodies such as the South African Institute of Chartered Accountants and the Independent Regulatory Board for Auditors have their hands full investigating the conduct of auditors. Those who are found guilty are struck off but the damage to investors is irreversible.

◆

In 2000 I left Deloitte to take up a position as head of the Financial Services Board (now the Financial Sector Conduct Authority), which regulates the entire financial services sector except for banks. I was the first black person to be appointed as head of the organisation.

When I arrived, the top management was lily white. One of my

---

[15] In December 2017, the CEO of the global furniture retailer Steinhoff, Markus Jooste, resigned in disgrace after auditors flagged accounting 'irregularities' in its books in what would turn out to be the biggest fraud in South African corporate history. VBS Mutual Bank was declared insolvent in 2018 after it was found that VBS managers and auditors, and businesspeople, as well as ANC politicians and EFF leaders, had stolen more than R2,7 billion from the bank. In 2019 a forensic investigation found some senior executives at Tongaat had allegedly been part of inflating the group's profits, with at least seven former senior officials of the company involved in the huge fraud and corruption case.

St Hubert Catholic church, where I was baptised, and the 'coloured school' where I completed the first three of my primary school years, both in Alexandra, are now heritage sites.

Newclare Primary School, 1960. Class photo – Standard 3 (Grade 5). I'm in the front row, third from the left. In the back row, fifth and seventh from the left, respectively, are Aubrey Brownley and Jakob Segelberg, who were involved in a tragic accident in which Jakob lost his life.

Chris J Botha High School reunion, 2003. I'm in the front, at the left. Next to me are my schoolmates Lynette Mooi and Lance Mooi, with Richard Page on the right. Another old classmate, Mercy Riechel, is in the back row (in the white tunic). Teachers who played important roles in my life included Reggie Feldman (in the back row wearing the red tie) and Brian Theron (to his right).

My brother Desmond with his dad Ali Buys and our mother Frances, 1963.

Oupa Hendrik in uniform in the Second World War.

Desmond's 3rd birthday, 1963. I'm on the left and Ephraim on the right.

Amy's and my wedding day, 1 June 1971.
Amy is with my mum Frances (left) and her
mother Francis.

He's in the army now, 1978.
Ephraim in his stepouts.

My daughters Althea
and Cheryl, 1979.
The Hillman was our
first family car.

Ouma Elsie, 1990s, with my mother Frances
(back, right) and Ephraim's daughters, Michelle
(back, left), Lesley Anne (front, left) and
Angrenaide.

Comrades Marathon, 1999. My third and best race.

Above left: Althea and her husband Tshidiso, with their daughters Tsholofelo (left) and Boitumelo.

Above right: Alvin graduates, 2011. With his proud parents.

Left: Cheryl and her husband Peter, with their twins Zac and Skylar, and daughter Jenna (in Cheryl's arms).

Below: Spanning the generations. Back row, from left: Boitumelo, myself, Althea and Tsholofelo. Front row, from left: Alvin, Skylar, Zac and Jenna.

On an MTN strategic planning trip to Silicon Valley, California, with Koosum Kalyan, Christine Ramon and Phuthuma Nhleko. What made an impression on me was how rapidly technology was changing the world and how the tech companies, from the behemoths to the start-ups, were willing to experiment without fear of failure.

Gareth Ackerman, Debra Muller, Haroon Bhorat, Bakar Jakoet and myself at Pick n Pay board function.

Above: Rick Cottrell, the transitioning chief executive of the Financial Services Board, the Minister of Finance, Trevor Manuel, and myself in 2000. This appointment is made by the finance minister and I was the first black chief executive in this position.

Left: At an Abasa function in honour of the newly qualified accountants in 2022, with Nondima and Wiseman Nkuhlu. Professor Nkuhlu has the honour of qualifying as the first black chartered accountant in the country.

Right: Some of the past presidents of Abasa, with the current president, Linda Maqoma, in 2022.

Back row, from left: Andile Khumalo, Lwazi Bam, Ashley Dicken, Sizwe Nxasana and Sathie Gounden.

Front row, from left: Futhi Mtoba, Tantaswa Fubu, myself, Linda Maqoma (president) and Gugu Ncube.

Left: A Finding the Fair Way Foundation workshop with a group of caddies to focus on their needs and concerns. A programme is in development to provide caddies with training about personal development, communication skills, financial wellness and the technical aspects of the game of golf.

From left to right: Kekeletso Rabotutu, Mervyn Jacobs, myself, Richard Mlambo, Matthews Sebetha, Obed Phundulu, Simon Mphahlele and Seth Naicker.

The value that a good caddy adds to a round of golf is invaluable and should be rewarded appropriately.

Fani Titi is part of my regular four ball.

Ralnick Turner, Norman Mbazima, myself and Thabo Khunyile about to tee off.

objectives was to ensure transformation, starting at the top and cascading throughout the organisation. To get this ball rolling, I split the roles of head of insurance and pensions into two – there was no logical reason why this position was combined, given the scope and complexity of each function – and promoted Dube Tshidi, a longserving employee, to head of the pensions division. A few years after I left, Dube was promoted to chief executive and excelled in that position.

I encouraged my friend, Mashudu Munyai, a chartered accountant, to apply for the position as head of insurance when that position became vacant. But my transformation drive wasn't sitting well with some of my colleagues, and Mashudu recalls that his resume mysteriously disappeared. When I saw that he wasn't on the list of potential candidates, I made some enquiries and his resume reappeared just as mysteriously. Mashudu smashed the interview, aced the psychometric tests, emerged as the top candidate and was duly appointed.

I also encouraged Jurgen Boyd, another chartered accountant, to apply for a top position in the financial markets division. After I left the Financial Services Board, Jurgen was promoted to head of the division.

Dube, Mashudu and Jurgen[16] were all well qualified and experienced: all they required was opportunity. When the opportunity arose, they grabbed it with both hands, excelled and made a

---

[16] Mashudu was stricken with cancer and sadly passed away in 2022. Dube and Jurgen have since retired.

significant contribution to the organisation.

One of the highlights during my tenure with the Financial Services Board was successfully piloting the Financial and Intermediary Services Act through parliament. This law aimed to professionalise the role of financial advisors in the industry. Before the law, any person, regardless of their qualifications or experience, could act as a financial advisor, often with disastrous consequences for investors. The law provided for the accreditation of financial advisors, based on qualifications and experience, which ensured significant protection for investors.

Another highlight was representing South Africa on the executive committee of the International Organisation of Securities Commissions (IOSCO), which regulates the world's securities and futures markets; I was also privileged to be elected as vice-chairman of IOSCO, with the support of the African-country members. And I represented South Africa as a trustee of the International Financial Reporting Standards Foundation, the global body responsible for accounting standards. On these international platforms, I always pushed not only the South African agenda, but the African agenda in general.

Throughout my career, whenever I was on a visit to any part of the African continent, I was welcomed and treated with love and respect, as a brother and fellow citizen. These were truly special moments that I will always treasure. It is a matter of pride for me that I managed to secure the respect and support of my African brothers and sisters.

9

PROFESSIONAL BODIES

As I've mentioned, I was blissfully unaware of the accounting profession when I was growing up. The only role models in my community were doctors, lawyers, teachers and salesmen.

After I qualified as a chartered accountant in 1981, I had a strong desire to contribute to the profession in one way or another, and my first priority was to promote the profession in the black community. I started visiting schools on career days to create awareness of the profession and encourage students to consider accounting as a career option. This was a mountain to climb, as being an accountant was considered to be the same as a bookkeeper, and not in the same category as the other professions.

Over the four years that followed, I managed to build a network of like-minded individuals who realised that successful economic growth and governance required sound accounting and efficient information systems; and that for the black population to participate effectively in the growth of the South African economy, it was crucial to develop their accounting capabilities. Most of them were still unqualified, but they all understood the need for us to collaborate in order to make a greater impact.

That was a difficult period. Throughout the 1980s there were great political upheavals, with hit squads on the loose, causing mayhem, and black-on-black violence on the increase. The future was uncertain and there was suspicion about almost everybody and everything.

In 1985 there was unprecedented hype created around what was billed to be a speech of great import by then state president PW Botha. It created much expectation both locally and abroad, with analysts suggesting that the white government was about to announce the ending of the 'kragdadigheid' (brute force) tactics it had been using against its opponents. But instead of announcing measures to ameliorate the jackboot governance of the time, Botha took the battle to those perceived by his National Party government to be enemies of the state. He announced that the country – his government – had adopted a 'Total Strategy' to forestall what he said was a 'Total Onslaught'.

It was in the midst of these uncertainties that we decided to establish a body that would represent the aspirations of black accountants, an organisation whose main objectives would be to address our needs. In 1985 we formed the Association for the Advancement of Black Accountants (Abasa) to address the inequalities in the accounting profession resulting from racial discrimination and to promote the professional interests of every black person engaged in or aspiring to the accounting profession. As there were so few qualified black chartered accountants at the time, we invited anyone who was associated with accounting work, including accounting technicians and aspiring accountants, to join the organisation. I was elected the founding president.

The timing of Abasa's establishment was fortuitous, coming when it was most needed. Those within the profession had been looking for answers to address their circumstances and had wanted to emulate their counterparts in the legal profession who earlier had started the Black Lawyers Association (BLA). Also up and running was the Black Management Forum (BMF), whose members were drawn mainly from the second and third tiers of management in the corporate sector – there were very few black managers in the first tier of management at the time. They were our role models, and included the likes of Godfrey Pitje and Dikgang Moseneke, members of the BLA, and Eric Mafuna, Martin Sebesho and Lot Ndlovu, all former presidents of the BMF.

Our first task was to engage the mainstream firms with a view to soliciting their support for the new body's programme, employing constructive engagement rather than an adversarial approach. And we figured it could only work to our advantage if we had support from the major global firms.

But the issues militating against black people qualifying as a chartered accountants had their origins at school level – the law and the design of the time, pre-1994, forced Africans to go to township schools, and to so-called 'bush colleges and universities' for their tertiary education. It was accepted that the standard of education in township schools and, to a lesser degree, at 'bush' universities was inferior to that of schools in the suburbs, and anyway most black universities didn't offer post-graduate degrees in accounting, a prerequisite for the qualifying examinations. Those who wanted to become chartered accountants first had to get their undergraduate degree, then proceed to so-called white universities for their post-graduate studies – but because they had studied at 'inferior' institutions, their applications were usually declined as it was presumed they wouldn't cope with a higher standard.

In order to overcome the established universities' rejection of black candidates, Abasa proposed to these institutions that a year's bridging course be provided in order to lift the standard and ensure that black students had an equal chance of success when they entered the main course.

◆

The security police were aware of Abasa and we were under constant surveillance: as all our political organisations were banned and our political leaders imprisoned, they thought we were merely a front organisation for political organisations, in particular the ANC.

In 1986 I became aware that my telephones at the office and at home were tapped. I received abusive phone calls all the time. If I travelled to Cape Town, as I often did, someone would call me up and tell me exactly where I'd stayed and where I'd gone – presumably the security police's way of making me aware that I was being followed.

I sought advice from Piroshaw Camay, the secretary-general of Nactu. Piroshaw was routinely picked up and jailed ahead of any declaration of a state of emergency by the apartheid regime. He wasn't very comforting: welcome to the club, he told me, and just try not to worry about them. I had no choice but to accept his advice.

SAICA was equally wary of us. They told us at the time that it would be best to work as a 'black interest group' under their auspices but we rejected this suggestion. We tried to reassure them that our aims weren't political but were centred on creating and promoting the accounting profession in our communities. However, when black business associations and other black professional bodies campaigned for Mandela's release, we joined the campaign – much to SAICA's dismay. This led to one of the SAICA executives threatening to have me struck off the roll for bringing the profession into disrepute. I disregarded the threat. (My relationship with SAICA has changed dramatically for the better since those early days.)

In the same year, we became aware of the National Association of Black Accountants in the USA. We suspected that they had similar challenges, as the major accounting firms had a global footprint, but they were at least 10 years ahead of us in terms of what they'd achieved for black American accountants, and we decided to make contact with them to see what we could learn. They welcomed the approach and invited us to their annual convention which was held that year in Dallas, Texas.

We scraped together the money, and Mashudu Ramano, who was the executive director of Abasa, and I set off for the convention. We were treated as very special guests and they rolled out the red carpet for us. We met the outgoing president, Ramona Henderson, the incoming president, Butch James, and committee members Linda Saulsby and Edwin Jenkins. They gave us a platform at the convention to talk about Abasa, and why we'd reached out to them.

We learned that they were at a point where they were being rec-ognised by global firms. They were starting to break through the barriers and many of their members had been made partners in major firms. They had career days to promote the profession in schools. They provided scholarships, established a forum to support emerging firms, and so on.

It was an emotional and unforgettable experience for us and we were determined to implement our learnings back home.

In 1986 we invited the National Association of Black Accountants to visit us in South Africa. We arranged a workshop at the Carlton Centre where they presented papers on various topics. We invited our members, guests from major firms and academia.

One of the attendees was Edwin Jenkins, who would go on to be managing director at JPMorgan Chase. 'Since US airlines couldn't fly direct to South Africa due to the US boycott of the South African government, I had to fly by night to London on a US carrier, spend the following day in the city and a hotel, and catch a night flight on British Airways to Nairobi, Kenya (I did not get off the airplane),' he recalls. 'I finally arrived mid-morning in Johannesburg. My rec-ollections of my arrival were the sight of soldiers with automatic weapons on the airport roof and behind sandbags on many street corners as my Abasa hosts (who picked me up at the airport) and I drove into Pretoria. I felt like I had entered into a military zone, which was not something I had ever experienced up to that point in my life – and I actually grew up in the segregated US state of Georgia.'

Despite this, Edwin says, he felt a 'tremendous welcome, warmth and respect from Abasa's members'. 'In a sense it was overwhelming. Despite the slavery my ancestors suffered and its continuing impact, which we still feel today in the US, I thought we Americans owed you respect for your endurance of apartheid and for the status Abasa had achieved at the time in South Africa. The one thing I felt, which I could not ever feel for myself as an American, was the belief that black South Africans would one day control their destiny as a people and the country of South Africa.'

Recalling that some of the themes of the convention were economic empowerment, and preparing Abasa for its role in helping shape the economic future, as well as the peaceful transition to black political control of South Africa, Edwin says that he 'noticed that the white businessmen were very engaging and respectful, and they seemed to understand apartheid would end in the not-too-distant future, and they would have to work with Abasa during the transition'.

When the attendees went to Johannesburg for a few days (where they saw a play at the Market Theatre and toured Soweto), Edwin says that although he felt the 'vibe for change was optimistic, apartheid was very visible through, for example, the bus depots with lines of people segregated by race, to the high fences around each and every home I saw in the designated white neighbourhoods.

'Abasa members were eager to learn from the Americans, but I honestly think we learned more from you,' Edwin concludes.

Linda Saulsby was another attendee. 'I am sure our facial

expressions and comments on the drive into Johannesburg [from the airport] demonstrated just how exceedingly naive we were about the country,' she recalls. 'Superhighway and skyscrapers lay ahead of us as we headed directly into downtown. We pulled up in front of a first-class hotel that rivalled any in the United States. The Carlton Hotel had begun to allow Africans and other people of colour as guests. In the past, the only people of colour seen in the hotel were, of course, its service personnel. We learned that the South African government had balked at the Carlton's decision, but after the hotel countered with a threat to divest its interests and withdraw from South Africa, the government relented.

'The conference, the first black-hosted event ever held in the Carlton Hotel, was attended by over seventy people. We were asked to lead a panel discussion that focused on the challenges of building their organisation and strategies for accelerating blacks in the accounting profession in a country that did not even regard them as fully participating citizens.

'I learned so much about South Africa, beyond the images that flash across television screens in America, that I often felt ignorant and uninformed. It was enlightening, exhilarating, intense and exhausting. I was constantly surprised, gladdened and saddened. The ingrained, almost fanatical focus on the division of the races and the huge, institutional bureaucracy that supported the policy of apartheid was even more insidious than I imagined. Hundreds of government employees, whose sole purpose was to record and monitor every South African by racial category, worked in a complex of sprawling buildings.

'The stark contrasts of quality of life and neighbourhoods, not only between whites and people of colour, but among the people of colour themselves – blacks, coloureds and Indians – underscored the reality of lives that were an excruciating combination of anger, resignation and accommodation. Coloureds and Indians could own land and homes, and many of their neighbourhoods resembled the average middle- or working-class neighbourhood in America; a few resembled America's upper-class communities, with big houses and manicured lawns. However, the overwhelming majority of blacks lived in poverty beyond description. A whopping 87 percent of the land in South Africa is rich and fertile, but all the black townships are located on the 13 percent of land that is not.'

Linda came to the conclusion that 'God had touched this tip of land in his universe'. 'He laid his hands on it and endowed it with a bounty of joys and sorrows,' she wrote. 'Its beauty, and abundance of natural resources embedded in fertile and mineral-rich land, is almost tragic in its proportion.' This is why, she concluded, everyone wants it and is willing to die fighting for it.

◆

The workshop was a huge success and suddenly opened doors for Abasa. We grabbed the opportunity to have one-on-one conversations with SAICA and the major firms, and the animosity that had initially greeted us disappeared. We began a new chapter in our relationships with our stakeholders.

Each year thereafter Abasa and the National Association of Black Accountants sent representatives to our respective annual conventions, which strengthened our relationships. At one such convention in Washington I was presented with an award for my contribution to the accounting profession in South Africa.

It was on one of these visits abroad that I met Tom Watson Jnr, a senior member of the National Association of Black Accountants and an early supporter of Abasa. I learned that Tom was a founder member of one of the largest black-owned accounting firms in the USA.

Tom visited South Africa on a number of occasions and often stayed with me and my family. Whenever I visited Washington, I would let him know in advance and make sure we got together for a catchup. I got to know Tom's wife, Paula Cholmondeley, also a chartered accountant and a member of the National Association of Black Accountants. Tom and Paula adopted a young black South African woman, Imogen Mkhize, who served a spell as executive director of Abasa.

Tom, a devout Muslim, felt that he had a higher purpose. He later left accounting to become a freelance writer, travelling around the world promoting his spiritual beliefs through fables and stories. He also told his inspiring and motivating stories at events hosted by Abasa. Yet Tom respected all religions and never tried to convert anyone to his faith.

In 1992, Tom described me (in USA McFarlane's New Africa News Service) as 'an instrument for social, economic and political change in South Africa'. 'He is making life better for his children, friends, colleagues and countrymen in his native land. He is a black man who is making a difference for us all.'

Tom noted that one of my favourite Bible stories is the story of Jonah. '[Jeff] says that he often feels like Jonah as he struggles for black economic empowerment in South Africa,' Tom wrote. 'As he tells the story, Jonah ran from God because he was afraid of the people's reaction to the message God wanted him to deliver. When he finally gave in and preached the message – telling the people to stop their evil ways and repent or be destroyed by God – the people repented and God did not destroy them.'

In the Bible story, Jonah was irritated that God had spared the people because he, Jonah, would have preferred to see them destroyed – he felt they deserved God's judgement. So Jonah then said to God in exasperation, 'I knew this would happen. That's why I did not want to carry your message.' Once he'd accomplished his assigned mission, Jonah was afraid that his countrymen wouldn't appreciate what he'd done for them.

'Jeff said he often has similar misgivings about carrying messages of change to white South Africans,' Tom wrote. 'Leadership is often thrust upon him. However, those asking him to lead often do not appreciate the personal risks he must take, nor do they appreciate what he has accomplished on their behalf. He is often like Jonah – a reluctant prophet/leader whose admonitions and warnings are followed so that the threats of dire consequences never are fulfilled. It is difficult for his countrymen to recognise or appreciate what he has done for them. He reluctantly takes on one leadership position after another, for the benefit of his countrymen, his successors and the world.'

◆

While initially our membership was restricted to black accountants only, whites were allowed to join from 1988 onward. The original name, the Association of Black Accountants of Southern Africa, was changed in 1991 to the Association for the Advancement of Black Accountants of Southern Africa, allowing for anyone who identified with the cause to join the organisation.

As I write this, Abasa is celebrating its 36th year. The successes that Abasa has achieved over the years are many. Almost all the major firms have black chief executives and at least half of the partners are black. When I qualified as a chartered accountant in 1981, to the best of my knowledge, there were three black (including coloured) chartered accountants in the country; I was the fourth. By 1992 there were more than forty black chartered accountants in the country. Today (2022), according to the records of SAICA, there are 9 389 black chartered accountants, representing 19.3 percent of the total number of chartered accountants in the country.

The immediate past president, Ashley Dicken, together with a young executive team, did amazing work – as have all the past presidents (see Appendix I). Many of them hold very prominent positions in business and the profession today. Linda Maqoma, who was on Ashley's executive team, has succeeded him as president and is continuing the excellent work.

◆

In 2018, during the tenure of president Gugu Ncube, I was invited to a meeting with the executive committee to explore the feasibility of establishing an investment arm of the organisation. The investment company would be a separate legal entity; Abasa would have a 49 percent stake and members of the organisation would be invited to become shareholders through a trust that would own the remaining 51 percent. The twin aims of the investment company was to create a new income stream for Abasa and promote a culture of saving for members.

Once we'd conceptualised the investment company, four of us crisscrossed the country, visiting branches and encouraging members to invest. We limited the maximum amount that anyone could invest to R150 000 because we wanted to spread the net as wide as possible. In the end, we were able to raise R1,2 million from members.

We then decided to do one more round of fundraising once we had identified a sound investment opportunity. Abasa Investments still has a pipeline of new opportunities that are being evaluated, and I have no doubt that some transactions will come to fruition in the near future.

10

KNOWLEDGE SHARING THROUGH
DIRECTORSHIPS

I was approached by mobile telecommunications company MTN in 2004 to consider taking on a non-executive director role. At the time I was the chief executive of the Financial Services Board. The JSE falls under the remit of the Financial Services Board, and MTN is a JSE-listed company; as such, I felt that I couldn't accept the position as I would be conflicted.

This got me thinking, though, and when I left the Financial Services Board in 2005, I decided it would be a good time to start a new chapter in my career as a non-executive director of listed companies.

Non-executive directors are members of the board of directors of a company or organisation, but not members of their executive management team; they're usually paid a fee for their services but they're not regarded as employees. Non-executive directors, who have the same legal duties, responsibilities and potential liabilities as their executive counterparts, provide independent oversight and serve on committees such as the audit and risk committee, the human resources and remuneration committee, the social and ethics committee, and the corporate governance committee. Most of the heavy lifting of boards is done in these committees.

I realised at the outset that being a board member was an onerous undertaking, and for this reason I felt that I wouldn't be able to do justice to more than three board positions.[17]

In 2006, I was once again approached by MTN and this time I accepted the position. At the time Cyril Ramaphosa, who has since become president of the country, was chairman of the board. The group president was Phuthuma Nhleko. I'd had some prior interaction with both Cyril and Phuthuma and we knew each other reasonably well. I felt privileged and honoured that they'd reached out to me. MTN was already one of the largest companies by market capitalisation on the JSE and boasted an impressive footprint across the rest of Africa and the Middle East.

As a chartered accountant, I was naturally appointed to the audit committee, where I remained until the end of my tenure. I was also appointed as chairman of the risk and compliance committee, a position I remained in for about seven years before resigning to join the human resources and remuneration committee. I later became a member of the finance committee and the social and ethics committee.

MTN was a complex group to manage. The company, primarily a provider of mobile services, had over the years morphed into a more diverse service provider which included financial and media services. Overseeing this diversification while ensuring the continued profitability of the business and keeping all the stakeholders, especially shareholders, happy was very demanding. Thankfully, the

---

[17] My attendance record as a director of listed companies is 100 percent over a period of 12-15 years.

board comprised local and international directors with considerable skills, knowledge and experience.

During my tenure at MTN there were many challenges. Two stand out. First were the heavy fines that the Nigerian government and revenue authorities attempted to impose on the company, and which we managed to either rebut or reduce quite substantially. The trouble had begun in 2015, when the Nigerian government tried to fine MTN the equivalent of US$5,2 billion after claiming it was continuing service to customers with unregistered SIM cards. The Nigerian Communications Commission later cut the fine by 25 percent. Another dispute started in 2018 when Nigeria said MTN owed the equivalent of $2 billion in unpaid duties and taxes; MTN denied the liability, and the Nigerian government finally dropped its case after 'careful review and due consultation with relevant statutory agencies'.

Second were the allegations of fraud regarding the licence awarded to Irancell, MTN's operating company in Iran. Turkcell, MTN's rival operator in Iran, accused MTN of bribery in obtaining its mobile licence for that country in a case it brought in the USA. The allegations were investigated thoroughly by the Lord Hoffmann committee, of which I was a member.[18] We found the allegations to be spurious.

I resigned from MTN at the end of 2019 after 13 years of service.

---

[18] The MTN board appointed two directors to the Hoffman committee, Peter Mageza and me. Neither of us had been on the board at the time the licence was awarded, and it was felt that we were not conflicted. This was canvassed with Lord Hoffman, who concurred.

◆

I've always admired Raymond Ackerman, who was often in the media because he was so successful. An iconic figure in South Africa, he had – and still has – a formidable reputation, having started Pick n Pay from a base of four small supermarkets in Cape Town some 55 years ago.

Today, it is one of the most successful retail companies, with a footprint not only in South Africa but in many other countries in southern Africa.

In the early days in the late 1960s, nothing was beyond Raymond, and he wouldn't hesitate to carry bags of groceries and packages to his customers' cars. His marketing was already legendary; as he built his business, for example, he would offer customers a facecloth if they spent R10, and a large slab of chocolate if they spent R20. Soft spoken, he always responded personally to correspondence.

So I was very excited when a headhunting firm approached me in 2007 about a potential appointment as a non-executive director of the company. The successful candidate was also to take over as chairman of the audit and risk committee. It was a great privilege and honour to be shortlisted for such a prestigious position.

David Robins, the deputy chairman, contacted me for an interview. I prepared well, combing through the company's latest annual report, familiarising myself with the numbers, the successes, failures and challenges. I also devoured Raymond's autobiography, *Hearing Grasshoppers Jump*, in which he deals with how he grew the business against strong competition from established retailers.

The interview went even better than I'd hoped. David has a warm and informal style and was easy to talk to. He then advised that the next step was for me to meet with Raymond himself. Even though I was a confident and experienced professional, this was a daunting prospect.

I met Raymond in his Kenilworth head office and together we walked to the boardroom for a discussion over a light lunch. To my surprise, I found the entire family – his wife Wendy, their sons Gareth and Jonathan, and their daughters Suzanne and Kathy – as well as David waiting for us. As we settled down for lunch, I braced myself for what I expected to be a tough session.

Within minutes, however, I realised that this family was very special. Despite their considerable wealth and stature, they were friendly and down to earth. The conversation was easy and free-flowing. The topics ranged from the personal, such as my family background, to corporate governance and my sense of where the company was at and where it was headed.

At the end of the conversation, Raymond offered me the job on the spot – and I immediately accepted.

The two challenges that stood out for me were, first, Pick n Pay's successful exit of the Franklins business in Australia; and, second, our successful unbundling of Pick n Pay Holdings.

Pick n Pay had initially entered the Australian market in 2001 via the acquisition of 86 Franklins stores, Australian discount super-markets selling groceries, perishables and 'no-frills' home-brand generic products. At the same time, Pick n Pay bought 20 Fresco supermarkets and rebranded them as Franklins stores. Pick n Pay was unable to achieve the necessary scale in a very competitive market and the returns were disappointing. For this reason, a decision was taken to exit Franklins and focus on the growth of the business in the rest of Africa.

The aim of the unbundling of Pick n Pay Holdings was to replace the 'pyramid' structure – introduced in 1981 by the Ackerman family to prevent a hostile takeover – with a simpler, more modern single share listing. The Ackerman family retained control of the business through the issue of B shares, with the approval of the shareholders.

When Hugh Herman, the longstanding lead independent non-executive director, stepped down from that position at the beginning of 2020, I was appointed as his successor. In 2022 the board recommended my reappointment as director for another year, subject to shareholder approval at the annual general meeting in July.

◆

In 2008 I was shortlisted by an executive search firm for the position of non-executive director and chairman of the audit committee of Exxaro Resources. Following a successful meeting with the nominations committee, I was appointed. I was subsequently appointed to the nomination and remuneration committee. When Len Konar, the chairman, resigned in 2018, I was appointed as his successor.

Two challenges stood out for me during my tenure. The first was Exxaro's acquisition of an iron-ore mine in the Republic of Congo.

After investing a total of about R5 billion, we decided to cut our losses and exit the business. Sadly, we lost our entire investment. Doing business in the rest of Africa isn't for the faint-hearted!

Second was Exxaro's diversification away from coal to renewable energy, mainly as a result of climate change. This diversification strategy is still at an early stage and I remain confident that it will be executed successfully in future.

I resigned from Exxaro in May 2021 after 12 years of service. Reflecting on my time at the company, I wrote in my farewell letter to the board, 'I think of all the amazing people that I have had the pleasure to work with over the years: people of all races and across gender and cultural divides. What has struck me almost from my very first encounter was just how incredibly dedicated and committed most of them were to the very profound vision of the company – empowering lives.'

It has been an amazing opportunity and privilege for me to work with some outstanding chairpersons and chief executive officers over the years. These include Cyril Ramaphosa, Phuthuma Nhleko, Mcebisi Jonas, Sifiso Dabengwa, Rob Shuter and Ralph Mupita at MTN, Raymond Ackerman, Gareth Ackerman, Nick Badminton, Richard Brasher and Pieter Boone at Pick n Pay, and Sipho Nkosi, Mxolisi Mgojo and Dr Nombasa Tsengwa at Exxaro. I was like a sponge, absorbing valuable lessons from these outstanding leaders.

◆

When I started my career as a non-executive director 15 years ago, black males and black females were generally not represented in the broader JSE-listed companies. Since then there has been a significant shift and numbers have increased dramatically. I predict that within the next 15 years whites will become the minority group. As this inevitable change gains traction, whites should embrace rather than resist change, as they will continue playing an important and meaningful role in business and the economy in general.

◆

I've always recognised the vital role that business plays in the economy, and by 2005 I was ready to step up and pursue my own entrepreneurial ambitions. I started my own business, Uranus Investment Holdings.

Over the years, Uranus has built a strong portfolio of investments following a strategy of acquiring investments and selling them at a profit in the future. The company takes minority stakes of between 10 and 25 percent in medium-sized businesses in mainly the financial services sector. (The company also had a stake in an IT company which it exited in 2019 at a healthy return on investment.)

When you overpay for an investment, it works against you in the medium to long term. For this reason we've walked away from many deals. And you run the risk of leaving a lot of money on the table if you're in a rush to exit. If the valuation doesn't make sense, we'd rather be patient and remain invested. We take as much care when we acquire an investment as we do when we exit one.

As a chartered accountant, I've been trained to consider financial ratios when evaluating investment opportunities. We typically examine the return on investment, return on capital employed, earnings yield, dividend yield and so on. However, this isn't where and how I start. In the first instance, I consider the values and principles of potential business partners. I do this through direct and face-to-face interaction. In most cases, I'm able to get a sense of who the people are during the first half hour of a meeting. If I sense that our values and principles aren't fully aligned, I'll seek a respectful way to cut the meeting short and that will be the end of it.

Two examples highlight this approach. The first was our investment in ICAP Holdings in 2006. At the time ICAP was a South African subsidiary of a London-based company listed on the London Stock Exchange.[19] I was introduced to the managing director, Koos de Klerk, by a mutual friend; I subsequently met two of the local directors, Wayne Jackson and Clint Valjallo; Bob Jones-Davies, the remaining director, was based in London and I was to meet him later on my trip there to meet with the global CEO.

From our very first contact, it was clear that the four of us were fully aligned when it came to values and culture. Uranus initially acquired a 15 percent interest in ICAP, followed by a further 6 percent a year later. The company graciously provided vendor funding at the prime rate of interest which meant that we were able to service the debt from the dividends paid by the company. We subsequently

---

[19] Since then there's been a merger in London and the company is now known as ICAP Tullets; it remains listed on the London Stock Exchange.

sold the 6 percent back to ICAP London and used the proceeds to pay out two of the co-founders of Uranus who had exited the business. The entire loan plus interest has since been repaid.

ICAP has enjoyed decent growth since we made our initial investment and remains profitable. Wayne and Clint – with whom my relationship has only strengthened over the years – with the help of Paul Wilson, the chief operating officer, are doing a sterling job of managing the business on a day-to-day basis. Koos and Bob have since retired.

The second example is Cornerstone Performance Solutions, a business started by Derek Shirley and his wife Karen about five years before we became involved. It's an education and training business which began with a focus on banking and has since diversified to other sectors of the economy.

Derek and Karen embody the true spirit of what it means to be entrepreneurs. They took the risk of forgoing the comforts of a corporate lifestyle to start their own business 21 years ago, and were smart enough to surround themselves with the most talented people.

At the time when we concluded the transaction in 2007, the business had reached a tipping point and was poised to take off. The valuation was based on the company's historical performance and did not really take its growth potential into account; for this reason we paid less than R500 000 for a 26 percent interest. We had the cash at the time and were able to pay the full amount upfront. We remain invested and have made a phenomenal return on our investment.

I subsequently learned from Derek that on the day we met to discuss a potential investment in the business, he and Karen had more or less decided to go with someone else. Derek told me that immediately after our meeting he called Karen to tell her not to sign with the other party.

While the aim of the initial investment may have been to enhance the black economic empowerment credentials of the company,[20] Karen says that the relationship has evolved way beyond this, and that all the directors (I am one of four) and shareholders operate as one big happy family and there are no colour lines. She says that I've added significant value to the growth of the business by applying my knowledge, skills and experience.

Today Cornerstone Performance Solutions is a very successful business. Derek and Karen have succeeded in creating value not only for themselves, but for all their stakeholders, including Uranus. Our relationship with them is based on honesty, mutual trust and respect, and will endure well beyond our business relationship.

◆

Uranus has had to deal with the normal strains and stresses of any new business, including disagreements between directors.

Uranus has broad-based shareholders, comprising doctors,

---

[20] 'Black economic empowerment' is a government policy that seeks to right the wrongs of the past and to distribute the wealth of the nation across all races and genders. A company's black economic empowerment 'credentials' can cover ownership, management control, employment equity, skills development, preferential procurement, enterprise development and socioeconomic development.

teachers and ordinary working people, who've invested about R1 million in the business. From the start, my own view of our business strategy was that all the capital invested by these minority shareholders had to be protected, and that the working capital had to be provided by the four founder members, including myself. To my dismay, I discovered that my co-founders didn't wish to risk any of their own capital beyond what they'd initially invested for their shares. This stance suggested that they weren't fully committed and had doubts about the long-term sustainability of the business.

Within two years, two of the co-founders had decided to exit due to these fundamental differences. We approached KPMG to value their stake in the business. Given that we'd only been in business for two years, I had a reasonable expectation that the valuation would come in at about R10 million. Between the two of them, those co-founders held 42 percent of the shares in business, which would amount to a payout of R4,2 million in total.

To my surprise, the valuation came in at R25 million. I often joke that if I ever wish to sell the business, I'll ask KPMG to do the valuation and become rich! I knew that there was no way that the KPMG valuation would stand up to independent scrutiny so I launched a court challenge.

On the day of the hearing, sanity prevailed and we settled on a valuation that was more aligned to what I thought the business was

---

[21] I lodged a complaint against KPMG with the Independent Regulatory Board for Auditors but, for reasons I don't understand, my complaint was dismissed. At that stage I had neither the desire, nor the energy or money, to continue the fight, and I decided to move on.

worth. My legal fees came to a whopping R1 million, which put severe strain on the cash flow, but the fight was worth it.[21]

Two years later the third founding member decided to exit the business and we were able to reach an amicable settlement without any legal dispute.

On reflection, I think the exiting of my co-founders was a blessing in disguise. It left me free to manage the business as I consider appropriate. And they all got their original investments back, plus a healthy return.

◆

Anyone who's ever started a new business knows that it's easier said than done. Research shows that 20 percent of new businesses fail in the first two years, 45 percent in the first five years and 65 percent in the first 10 years. Only 25 percent make it to 15 years or more. Thankfully, Uranus falls into this last category.

Being in business means having a medium to high appetite for risk – it's certainly not for the faint-hearted. No matter how prudently you approach a potential transaction, there's always risk involved, and some businesses will fail. Uranus has had its share of failures and has lost about R3 million over the years. Thankfully, our successes dwarf our losses.

Since Uranus was established in 2005, the business landscape has profoundly changed. The financial crisis of 2008 seriously threatened the sustainability of businesses across all economic sectors, irrespective of size and longevity. Many businesses were unable to weather the storm and were bankrupted. Some highly leveraged companies were unable to service debt and went bust. Others, including Uranus, were able to survive that challenging period and remain on a sound financial footing.

In 2020, the business landscape once again experienced unprecedented economic and social disruption due to the covid-19 pandemic and the various lockdowns that followed. The impact of covid-19 on the economy has been devastating. Sadly, many small businesses have gone bankrupt, an unprecedented level of retrenchments has ensued, and unemployment has soared.

The government has attempted to soften the impact on the poor and vulnerable by introducing a 'special grant' of R350 per month, but these measures aren't sustainable because of an already overstretched fiscus. Nonetheless, history has shown that we are a resilient nation. We've been through worse and we will get through this crisis.

The businesses within the Uranus investment portfolio have also shown remarkable resilience and have not only weathered the storm but have emerged much stronger. As a consequence, Uranus business remains in a sound solvency and liquidity position. Under my watch, our minority shareholders have quadrupled their initial investments, and been repaid half this value by way of dividends, while the other half remains invested in the business.

I remain focused on building the business. There will always be exciting new opportunities to invest in and grow the business in future.

11

FIT BODY, FIT MIND

Much of my life has been consumed by work – I've spent more time on work than on anything else. This has, of course, been stressful, but stress builds up very slowly over time and we're often unaware of just how strung out we are. As most of us know, stress manifests in various ways – poor sleeping patterns and being short-tempered, for example.

I think it's fair to say that my hobbies of, initially, road running and, later, golf were what kept me healthy – and sane.

During the mid-1990s, I was an avid runner and I would often bump into a neighbour, Mashudu Munyai, on the road, and we would complete our runs together – we lived fairly near each other in Fourways. Eventually we arranged to run together.

I first met Mashudu when we were both active within Abasa, and he was passionate about sharing his knowledge and experience with young aspirant accountants. He encouraged me to join the Rand Athletic Club and I started running weekend road races with him all across the country. I ran my first standard marathon of 42 kilometres with Mashudu as my coach. At the 32-kilometre mark I hit the proverbial wall and wanted to give up. Mashudu gently coached me through the pain and exhaustion, and I ended completing the run in less than four and a half hours.

I was so encouraged by this that I ended up running more than 30 marathons between 1997 and 2014, including 20 standard marathons, the Two Oceans six times, the Comrades four times, and the New York, Paris and London marathons. If it hadn't been for Mashudu, I would never have experienced the joys of long-distance running.

It's interesting to note that two decades before I became interested in road running, my friend and colleague at Schwartz Fine, Bernie Fridman, ran the Comrades unofficially in protest against the 'white males only' restriction on participation. 'We discussed this injustice many times,' Bernie recalled in a later conversation with me, 'and it troubled me. With your support, I tried to organise a boycott of the race through letters to the press.'

Sadly, we discovered that the marathon public at large weren't interested in a boycott. The apathy, lack of empathy and indifference of the other runners at the time were hard to understand but sadly not uncommon. That's why Bernie decided to run the 1974 race unofficially – along with several people of colour who were following in the footsteps of Robert Mtshali, who in 1935 had become the first black runner to cross the Comrades finish line unofficially. 'You supported this idea and with your support I felt I was doing the correct thing,' he told me. The run was highly publicised in the English press at the time.

'I didn't get a medal even though I finished in about six and a half hours and, similarly, the other athletes of colour who finished the race unofficially didn't get medals.'

In 1975 the Comrades was opened up so that people of colour and female athletes could participate. Thirty-five years later, in 2010, the Comrades Marathon Association finally awarded Bernie his silver medal. It's embedded in the wall at the entrance to Comrades House in Pietermaritzburg. The plaque reads, 'This silver medal was finally presented to Bernard Fridman in April 2010 and now symbolises a free, fair and just Comrades Marathon.'

Some of my other mates with whom I've had memorable runs include Violet Ricketts, Joe Morris (we ran the Paris and London marathons together in 2009 and 2012 respectively), the late Pat Ward and the late Shariefa Nieftagodien, and Richard Page. In fact, my most memorable run was the one I did with Richard in 2001 – the New York City Marathon.

He and I had decided early that year that we'd join a group of runners from Rand Athletic Club on a trip to the USA to run the race. In preparation for the trip, Richard and I entered the London Marathon in April, and we both ran well, which gave us confidence. We applied for passports and visas, booked our hotel and paid the entry fees. We were very excited and couldn't wait for the event.

On 11 September 2001 images of an attack by al-Qaeda terrorists against the USA flashed across our television screens. One aeroplane had been flown into the north tower of the World Trade Centre in lower Manhattan; another hit the south tower. Both towers collapsed less than two hours later. A third flight was hijacked and crashed into the west side of the Pentagon. A fourth was flown in the direction of Washington DC and crashed in a field near Shanksville, Pennsylvania. The attacks resulted in almost 3 000 fatalities and over 25 000 injuries. We were shocked and saddened.

Some weeks later, there was speculation in the media that the race, scheduled for November, would be cancelled. The New York City Marathon is very popular, attracting tens of thousands of runners from all over the world. The 42-kilometre route goes through the five boroughs of New York, and there was naturally concern that terrorists may attempt to somehow sabotage the race, for example by blowing up the bridges connecting the boroughs.

Ultimately, the organisers, with the support of then New York mayor Rudy Giuliani, decided to proceed with the race. They wanted to send a strong message that New York would stand up to terrorists – a show of strength and resilience. The mayor assured runners that there would be a strong security presence and that the risks were minimal.

While a few members of the Rand Athletic Club group pulled out due to safety concerns, most of us decided to proceed. It was our way of showing support and solidarity.

On the day, almost 25 000 runners lined up at the start. There was certainly a strong security presence and Giuliani was there to welcome us; he made special mention of foreign runners of which there was a very strong contingent. The race went off smoothly, with no incidents, and Richard and I finished in our target time of under four and a half hours.

Later we visited the site of the attack, where we could still see signs of smoke from the fire that had engulfed the buildings – it took over three months after the suicide attacks for the final fires to stop burning at what became known as 'Ground Zero', and acrid clouds of smoke from the site could be smelled several kilometres away in Brooklyn and upper Manhattan. The fires, fuelled by documents and office furniture, needed a near-constant jet of water sprayed on them. Excavation work was underway and by the time Richard and I visited, it was unlikely that any more survivors would be found.

I spent a few more days in New York City with Edwin de Broize, the brother of Joseph de Broize, a good friend and running mate of mine. Edwin, who'd immigrated to the USA and become a citizen, invited me on a club run with his mates, who were in awe that I'd made the trip all the way from South Africa to run the race under such difficult circumstances. The camaraderie, warmth and hospitality I experienced hanging out with this group of runners was amazing.

◆

By the time I was in my early 60s I felt that the running was getting a bit much on my body and decided to migrate to golf. The sport has since played a major role in my life, not only because of the friends I've made through it, but also for philanthropic reasons.[22]

In 2014 I employed the services of Michael Dreyer, a professional

---

[22] The South African Professional Golfers Association estimated in 2009 that golf contributed R58,4 billion to the South African economy. In 2021, 12 years later, a good guess is that amount is about R100 billion. I, like many people, have always considered golf to be a sport for the elite. For a start, it's very expensive – a bag of decent clubs easily costs more than R20 000, and new golf balls cost up to R70 each. But while it's true that the elite are attracted to the game, many golfers are from the middle class.

golfer, to teach me the ropes. I played that first round at the Country Club Johannesburg, of which I'd been a member since 1992, and which boasted two impressive golf courses, Woodmead and Rocklands, at its campus in Woodmead (it has another campus in Auckland Park).[23] I found it hard going and was absolutely exhausted at the end of the round.

Golf is by no means an easy game! Some of my friends say that they have tried and given up; they've either given away their golf clubs or they're collecting dust somewhere in the garage. I apparently have a higher threshold for pain and suffering and tend to persevere, and I've worked hard over the years to improve my game. My handicap at the moment varies between 18 and 24, depending on the difficulty of the course.

---

[23] I'm also a member of the CMR Golf Club and the Soweto Golf Club, the only two clubs in Johannesburg where black members are in the majority.

PART 4

———— ❖ ————

PAYING IT FORWARD

*'The most precious gift we can offer anyone is
our attention. When mindfulness embraces those we love,
they will bloom like flowers.'*

Thich Nhat Hanh

I2

STANDING UP FOR THE CADDIES

One of the first people I met on the course when I began playing in 2014 was a caddie called Benedict Bapela, who'd worked for the club for almost 20 years. He and I became good friends and, along with some other caddies (many of them from nearby Alexandra, the place of my birth), like Sipho Tshona, Lucky Peters, Carel Mabuza and Victor Mashila, we sometimes played golf together and had lots of fun.

When caddying for me, Benedict and the others had to work very hard to start with, because they were always looking for my golf balls. They also helped me enormously, teaching me how to swing the club, which club to use depending on the distance required or the lie of the ball, and how to putt. Benedict, who advised me not to try to kill the ball, would be ruthlessly honest when I asked him how I was doing, and tell me I was terrible.[24]

Mashudu Munyai, who'd been such a steadfast running mate for me, was also a keen golfer, and we enjoyed playing together until he was stricken with cancer.[25] And I met my friend Fani Titi during our stint as directors of MTN, when we discovered that we'd both recently started playing golf and were very passionate about it. Our

---

[24] When Benedict was diagnosed with cancer in 2019, I visited him before he died, at his home with his wife and two daughters, and he reminded me of how badly I putted, and how noisy and excited I was when I sank a putt, and we both laughed.

[25] Mashudu passed away in January 2022. I was fortunate to visit him twice in his last week in the hospital.

friendship has endured beyond MTN, and to this day, Fani and I, together with two close friends, Norman Mbazima and Thabo Khunyeli, play regularly as a four-ball.

As important to me, however, is the 'giving back' element of the game. One pathway for this is the Queen Butterfly Foundation, founded by Palesa Mofokeng to take care of severely handicapped children. I first met her when, in 2015, I was invited to play at a charity golf day at Ruimsig Golf Course, and she approached me as I was getting my golf bag out of the car to ask me how to go about arranging a fundraising golf event.

My investment company, Uranus, has since sponsored many fundraising golf events and facilitated numerous donations to the foundation from friends and business associates. I've visited the organisation many times over the years and I'm always touched by the children I meet and the staff who take care of them with such loving attention – it takes a special kind of person to do this sort of work. I have a beautiful painting in my office painted by the children as a gift to me which I will cherish forever.

◆

As a regular player at various courses across the country, and often as a friend of the men and women who caddied for me, I observed that the working conditions of golf caddies left much to be desired. Caddies weren't employed by the clubs, as most golf players assumed; they were regarded as self-employed or 'independent contractors'.

Simply on the basis of this unfair label, caddies have been denied full labour rights for more than a century. While it's understandable that this practice, first introduced by the British during colonial times, could survive during the apartheid era, there's nothing to justify it still being in place today, 27 years into democracy.

For their income, caddies rely on being lucky enough to get a bag, which means caddying for a golf player – carrying their bag, keeping the clubs clean, and walking ahead to locate balls and calculate distances to the pin and/or hazards. At the end of the round, the player pays the caddie the minimum suggested fee set by the club, which ranges from about R150 to R250 for a round of 18 holes. Most players stick to the minimum fee set although a few pay a bit extra.

Caddies often arrive at the clubs by 5am in the hope of getting a bag. Some clubs provide them with some tea or coffee and bread in the morning while others don't. If they don't get a bag, that's all they'll have to eat for the day. They often don't have the money for transport, and will walk to and from clubs; and even if they do get a bag, they'll often walk home in the afternoon to save money. Getting a bag sometimes goes along with a food voucher from the club which allows for a meal during the day from the staff canteen; in some instances, the players give the caddies money (usually about R50) to buy food.

Most of the caddies are family men and women. They have spouses and children who depend on them, and the same kind of day-to-day expenses as other people, such as groceries, rent, electricity, school fees, uniforms and stationery.

It's a fact that white citizens of this country have never been deprived of their rights, while black citizens were denied basic rights under colonial and apartheid rule – so when the white management of most clubs tell the black caddies that they have no employment rights, it touches a very raw nerve.

Over the years I've tried to engage with the management of various clubs with a view to improving the working conditions of their caddies. To my dismay, I discovered that most of the clubs didn't care much at all, holding the view that they were doing the caddies a favour by allowing them onto the golf course to carry bags. The clubs felt they had no legal responsibility towards the caddies and that the caddies ought to be grateful to have a job.

I was always appalled by this callousness, which finds personification in the sad story of the late Bongani Khumalo. Bongani worked as a caddie at Leeuwkop Golf Club for more than 20 years. In the last few of those years, he was granted permission by the club to go into the dams on the golf course to retrieve golf balls to sell second-hand. I often play at Leeuwkop and was one of Bongani's customers; I told him how I admired his work ethic, as we'd often see him neck-high in the water, using his feet to find golf balls. Bongani would also scale the fence at Randpark Golf Club at night and go into the dams there in his quest for golf balls.

One early Monday morning, Bongani's body was found next to a dam at Randpark. It's unclear what had happened: his clothes were neatly folded next to him, alongside 34 golf balls he'd retrieved during the night. It was left to Bongani's eldest daughter, aged 19, to bury her father.

When I learned about these tragic events, I approached the manager of Leeuwkop to try and establish what assistance they could provide to the family. The manager was quite clear that the club had no responsibility to him as Bongani was not in their employ.

Uranus covered the funeral costs.

◆

The results of a study conducted by the National Institute of Occupational Health on the working conditions of caddies at six golf clubs in Johannesburg were released in February 2019. The findings, which were widely circulated in the golfing establishment, were worse than anticipated, and included the fact that caddies experience income and food insecurity, high stress levels, alcohol and drug abuse, and muscular and skeletal problems arising from carrying heavy golf bags over long periods. There's no safety net for caddies when they fall ill or are injured and unable to work; they have no unemployment insurance, no medical aid and no retirement fund.

The management of the clubs undertook to address the issues raised as a matter of urgency, but by the end of 2020, there was no discernible change in the working conditions of caddies at these clubs, or anywhere in the country, for that matter. So, in partnership with film producer Rob Shermbrucker, I decided to do a documentary to create awareness of the plight of caddies. During the filming, Clovelly Country Club in Cape Town signed employment contracts with some of their caddies, breaking with a century-old employment practice within the golf establishment.

The film, *Finding the Fair Way*, was released in March 2021. While it was well received by many, others felt it shamed the golf industry by focusing only on the negative aspects of the sport. Clovelly Country Club again made the tough decision to embrace rather than resist change, and provided the link to the documentary to all their members and encouraged them to view it. By so doing they not only acted in the best long-term interests of their members, but also enhanced the brand and reputation of the club. This was the response that Rob and I had hoped and prayed for.

During April 2021, however, Country Club Johannesburg decided to reduce the number of their caddies from 115 to 88, effectively retrenching 27 people. It's worth mentioning that, despite the timing of this action during the covid-19 pandemic, the global health issue had nothing to do with the club's decision: they merely felt there were too many caddies and that 88 was the optimum number, arguing – quite correctly – that fewer caddies would result in more bags for those remaining. The club said that this retrenchment would be done on a voluntary basis and offered an inducement of R25 000 to every caddie who took up the offer.

Although I was an elected member of the country club's governing body, I wasn't consulted by the management and wasn't party to this inducement offer. The decision was made by executive management and approved by the golf committee; management then tabled the decision with the governing body of which I was a member, but for noting only. The caddies had made me aware of the decision a few days before the meeting, and had complained that they had not been consulted and were bitterly unhappy, so I was shocked when management informed us that they had consulted the caddies and that the caddies were happy!

I was approached for advice by the elected representatives of the caddies, Matthews Phakathi, Matthews Sebetha, Simon Mphahlele, Raymond Mshamba, John Mhambi, Lucas Mkhwanazi, Richard Malambo and Obed Phundulu. These men, all caddies at Country Club Johannesburg for many years, take their responsibilities very seriously; showing little concern for themselves, they're sharply focused on the best interests of those they represent. The fact that they're able and prepared to stand up for their rights against a very powerful management speaks, in my opinion, to their strength of character and integrity.

I found myself in an awkward position, so when I agreed to assist the caddies, I declared my conflict of interest and resigned from the club's governing body by mutual agreement.

The caddies felt the inducement offer wasn't acceptable for a number of reasons, prime among which were that they hadn't been consulted, and that the amount offered didn't take into account the years of service rendered, bearing in mind that some caddies had been on the job for more than 40 years.

I advised the caddies that they should obtain legal advice and undertook to either source funding or pay for it myself. The legal advice was that there was a fifty-fifty chance that a court would find that the caddies were employees in terms of the Labour Relations

Act. Such a finding would entitle them to all normal benefits including a salary, annual leave, sick leave and medical aid.

We reached a settlement with Country Club Johannesburg on the basis that they would pay those caddies who wished to retire R33 500 each, including R6 000 to cover a funeral policy for 10 years. A total of 35 caddies, including those who only worked weekends, decided to take up the offer; many of these were old, frail and in poor health, and desperate to retire.

To determine the employment status of golf caddies, we engaged with the director-general of the Department of Labour to identify loopholes in the Labour Relations Act 66 of 1995 and close them. At the time of writing, we'd established that the law provides 'a rebuttable presumption' that the caddies are employees, which puts the onus on the clubs to prove otherwise; and also that the caddies are protected under the National Minimum Wage Act. We sent the response from the Department of Labour detailing these two points to national golfing body GolfRSA, as well as the presidents of all the golf unions in the country, and asked for a meeting to discuss the way forward. At the time of writing, this process was ongoing.

While all this was going on, I made a submission on behalf of Uranus to the Minister of Justice in support of the Promotion of Equality and Prevention of Unfair Discrimination Amendment Bill. The Promotion of Equality and Prevention of Unfair Discrimination Act was originally passed in 2000, to serve as a comprehensive anti-discrimination law prohibiting unfair discrimination by the government and by private organisations and individuals. I pointed out that, despite this, increasingly unfair and discriminatory behaviour and practices are being seen in both the public and private sectors, mainly because of the weaknesses and shortcomings of the Act.

◆

Following on the success of the *Finding the Fair Way* documentary, Uranus facilitated the establishment of the Finding the Fair Way Foundation, the main objectives of which include providing caddies' training, providing educational support to the children of caddies, alleviating hardship when caddies are unable to work due to illness or injury, and providing access to alternative employment opportunities.

On 10 March 2022, the foundation held its inaugural golf day at Country Club Johannesburg, partly to enhance awareness of the plight of caddies, but also to raise funds to assist the caddies with hearing aids and spectacles – they can't perform their tasks properly if they're unable to hear the instructions of the players or see the ball flight.

A total of 43 caddies got bags on the day, paid for by the foundation at 60 percent above the standard fees. In addition, 16 caddies from four golf courses played in the event as full participants – unprecedented in the 100-year history of the club.

There was, however, an unfortunate fallout following this wonderfully successful event. Around June 2021, a couple of months before we established the Finding the Fair Way Foundation, I'd been approached by Dinky Morapane, an avid golfer and a member of Country Club Johannesburg, who told me that he'd heard about the work I was doing for the caddies and wanted to help. I was very grateful for his offer, and in various ways he indeed proved helpful in moving the process along.

When we registered the foundation, it was certainly my intention to appoint Dinky as a director but for reasons that aren't clear to me, he failed to provide the supporting documents required.

Following the successful golf day in March 2022, and completely out of the blue, Dinky suddenly accused all the foundation's directors of fraud and corruption. We were left with no choice but to instruct our lawyers to issue summons against Dinky for damages in order to protect our names and reputations. While this matter is likely to come to trial long after this book is published, we're confident that we'll be fully vindicated.

13

GIVING BACK

When I was in Grade 10 at Chris J Botha High School, and a keen and successful student, my family found they could no longer cope with the burdens of funding school uniforms, transport and food. It looked seriously as if I'd have to drop out of school.

It was my commerce teacher, Brian Theron, who witnessed my distress and stepped in. He asked me to come to his classroom, where he pulled some bursary application forms from his drawer. Together, we filled them in. My application for financial assistance to the City of Johannesburg was successful, and the bursary was renewed for Grades 11 and 12.

Who knows what might have happened if it hadn't been for Brian's intervention? What makes this particularly poignant is that I learned later that Brian came from a similarly disadvantaged background.

In 1990 when I was made a partner at Deloitte, the firm hosted a welcome function for me at the Carlton Hotel. One of my special guests was Brian. It was an opportunity for me to thank him for helping me when I needed it most.

◆

The knowledge I gained through my studies and subsequent work experience afforded me great opportunities, and these in turn led me to the privileged position of being able to give back, something

I'm very passionate about.

Some people have a philosophy of taking care of themselves first, and there's nothing wrong with that. I'm not being judgemental, as I recognise that we're not all wired the same way. My personal philosophy, which has been deeply influenced by the lessons I learned growing up, is helping others as I climb. This means that while I've pursued goals such as forging a career or building a business, I've reached out at the same time to extend a helping hand to others. Over the years I've helped many worthwhile causes, a few of which I detail here.

The *Riverlea Development Trust* was established in 2006 by Riverlea's community leaders, in response to the findings of a health, environment and development study, under the auspices of the World Health Organization between 2005 and 2010, which showed a welter of problems in the area. The trust has since embarked on a number of interventions to alleviate the plight of the community, including a national campaign against hookah pipes, promoting and funding cottage industries, providing tablets to unemployed youth to help them search for jobs online, and connecting unemployed youth with employment agencies and companies such as Pick n Pay. The trust also supports individual families in events of hardship where required.

In 2009 I contacted Brian once again and mooted the idea of establishing an education fund to help students in need of financial assistance. Brian, together with Hilton Mayet, another past teacher at Chris J Botha High, helped establish the *Reggie Feldman*

Education Trust, named after the vice-principal and my English teacher at CJB. The main aim of the trust is to promote a culture of learning and provide bursaries to scholars from primary school to college. Over the years Uranus has made direct funding available as well as leveraged its network and relationships to provide support. When I retired from the MTN board in 2019, for example, the company made a donation of R100 000 to the trust in my name. Since its inception, the trust has raised in excess of R1 million, all of which has been spent on supporting students in one way or another.

Then *Newgen Academy* was founded in 2017 by businessman Melvin Watkins, businesswoman Sherall Tasak and former school principal Anthony Swartz. When Uranus invested in the school in 2018, I was appointed to the board. Newgen is the only private school in Eldorado Park. Self-funding, it receives no money from the government. There are currently 434 learners. In 2020, 33 of them wrote matric and the pass rate was 85 percent, an improvement of the previous year's 75 percent pass rate.

In 2018 Uranus entered into an agreement with a UK-based company to market an online mathematics learning tool for Grades 1 to 9 called *10 Ticks Mathematics* in South Africa. Uranus then partnered with Teach SA, a non-profit organisation, who established sound relationships with the teachers and learners and facilitated workshops in all the schools. There were some outstanding results in a few cases but, in general, schools struggled to obtain an average mark of 30 percent in mathematics: teachers weren't computer literate and struggled with the online teaching, while learners didn't have access to computers and/or wifi; the government was either unable or unwilling to provide the necessary support. Sadly, the challenges were insurmountable and the project was abandoned.

The *South African Music Competition Trust* was established in 2012 to showcase musical talent, hosting a number of successful competitions for church choirs from Eldorado Park, Ennerdale, Bosmont, Riverlea, Newclare, Noordgesig and Coronationville. The covid pandemic made it impossible to continue, but the competitions will start again when the danger has passed.

In 2021 I was appointed a trustee of the *Unisa Foundation Trust.* I'm honoured to play a role in the trust of my alma mater and help the university raise funds in pursuit of its strategic goals and objectives.

◆

The political and business landscape in South Africa is very different today than it was three decades ago. Although we are still struggling with the legacy of the twin evils of colonialism and apartheid, black people in general and black businesses in particular have made and continue to make huge strides in all spheres of society.

To put these advances into perspective, let's go back to 1990, the year that Dr Ben Vosloo, the managing director of the Small Business Development Corporation, arranged a fact-finding mission to a number of countries, which I went along on. We were accompanied by Dr Nthato Motlana, a leading figure in many anti-apartheid organisations. On this very rewarding trip, which yielded plenty of ideas and suggestions around how to stimulate the growth and development of small businesses, we visited Moscow and Saint Petersburg in Russia, Malaysia, and New Delhi and Mumbai in India.

This wasn't the only global fact-finding mission I went on. During the period of 1989-1993, Willie Ramoshaba, a founder member and vice-president of Abasa during my tenure as president, arranged several business missions to other countries, including Malawi, Zimbabwe and the USA. I was privileged to be part of the mission to the USA led by Dr Nthato Motlana, and which included other prominent leaders such as Dr Ellen Kuzwayo, the life president of the National Black Consumers Union, James Ngcoya, president of the South African Black Taxi Association, and Solomon 'Stix' Morewa, general secretary of the Soccer Association of South Africa.

Dr Motlana noted in the mission brochure that 'no other country in the world epitomises the spirit of free enterprise as does the United States of America', despite the 'sometimes severe criticisms that have accompanied their success story'. The mission there, he said, was 'to study at first hand how your system works – we come from a country where a racial oligarchy created a socialist welfare system for the whites and virtually enslaved the blacks to subservience. We blacks are thus without an entrepreneurial culture'. He wrote, 'Black South Africans are looking forward to role models in developed countries with large black populations – since these are almost entirely absent in their fatherland. On our visit to the United States we hope to learn from both black and white Americans how to turn the 80 percent of our people who have always been job-seekers into creators of jobs and wealth.'

In 1990, the Aspen Institute, a USA-based think tank, invited me to present a paper at a conference about South Africa held in Bermuda. The delegates were mainly USA senators and congress-men, while the South African speakers were drawn from all spheres of society, including politics, academia, labour and business. It was a huge learning experience for me. It was also a wonderful oppor-tunity for me to interact with and debate various issues with my fellow citizens – with whom I had very little or no contact at home.

When Nelson Mandela was released, the Aspen Institute arranged for a follow-up conference in Cape Town to which I was also invited. I had the privilege of listening to Mandela's presenta-tion and was enthralled by the ensuing debate. What struck me forcibly at the time was the respect Mandela commanded and the humility he displayed in interacting with these powerful politicians. There was no doubt that Mandela was held in very high esteem and I felt proud to be a South African.

In 1993, a year before the ANC came to power, Willie Ramoshaba arranged a business summit in the Kruger National Park to dis-cuss the role of black business in a post-apartheid South Africa. For the first time in the history of black business, 200 delegates from all the organised business and professional bodies came together, along with 60 members of the ANC, the government in waiting.

Their delegation included Cyril Ramaphosa, Saki Macozoma, ANC spokesman at the time and currently a leading businessman, Trevor Manuel, who later became finance minister, and Tito Mboweni, who became Minister of Labour and later the Governor of the South African Reserve Bank. The agenda included affirmative action, financial and development institutions, international development agencies, privatisation, anti-trust legislation and unbundling of conglomerates, combating violence, and the role of black business in the forthcoming elections.[26]

◆

During the election campaign in the run-up to South Africa's first free election in 1994, the ANC campaign slogan was 'A better life for all'. This slogan resonated very powerfully with me. I considered it not merely a motto to win votes but a genuine commitment to bring about profound change. I felt that all South Africans would readily embrace rather than resist change, and work together to create a better life for all of our people.

In 1996, when Stella Sigcau, Minister of Public Enterprises in Nelson Mandela's cabinet, approached me to become her special advisor, I jumped at the opportunity. This was my chance to work

---

[26] Many of the recommendations yielded by this conference flowed through to the Reconstruction and Development Programme embarked on by the ANC when they came to power in 1994. A follow-up summit was held in 1999 to review the progress made at the end of the ANC's first term in power. Again, many of the recommendations flowed through to the economic policies of the government in subsequent years. Willie is planning yet another summit in the near future which will focus primarily on unemployment and job creation.

with the new government to help bring about meaningful change in the lives of back people who had endured so much under apartheid. My firm, Deloitte, seconded me to Sigcau on a full-time basis and I remained in that position for two years.

During my tenure as special advisor, I realised that the state-owned enterprises, which fell within the minister's remit, were very poorly run. This had been the practice under the apartheid government for decades, and the culture of poor governance and wasteful expenditure was deeply embedded. At the same time, it was very clear to me that privatisation was a bridge too far. The Congress of South African Trade Unions (Cosatu), as a member of the tripartite alliance – an agreement of political alignment forged in 1990 between the ANC, Cosatu and the South African Communist Party – was vehemently opposed to privatisation, and for this reason the government wouldn't consider it. At best, there was agreement that the state-owned enterprises required some drastic restructuring to enhance efficiency and reduce dependence on government funding, including guarantees, to keep them going.

At one stage, the minister asked me to accompany her to a meeting with President Mandela in his office at the Union Buildings to discuss the restructuring of state-owned enterprises. This was the first time I was in close proximity to the president and I was, naturally, intimidated. Somehow I managed to maintain my composure, however, and the minister asked me to brief the president on the governance protocol we planned to put in place to enhance the efficiency of state-owned enterprises. The plan included appointing well-qualified and experienced directors, reducing reliance on government funding, empowering the boards and limiting government interference.

The president asked very penetrating questions, including about the implications for staff and particularly the potentially negative impact on employment levels. The minister and I assured him that we would approach the restructuring of state-owned enterprises in a pragmatic and disciplined manner, and that staff numbers would be gradually reduced over time through natural attrition.

The minister and our team tried extremely hard to implement these changes but had limited success – ideological differences, cadre deployment and the government's inability to refrain from interfering stymied our best efforts. There was lack of financial discipline and no appetite for managing expenses or for achieving a reasonable level of profitability – and, as we all know, any business that fails to make a profit isn't sustainable.

Sadly, as we've learned from the judicial commission of enquiry into allegations of state capture, corruption and fraud – known to most South Africans as 'the Zondo Commission', after Judge Raymond Zondo, who headed it – the governance of state-owned enterprises has worsened since then, and endemic mismanagement and corruption are pervasive.

During the first year of my tenure with Stella Sigcau, I was accused of corruption by an official in the department, a career civil servant employed by the previous apartheid government and who now found himself accountable to a black female minister. My accuser leaked his false information to a daily newspaper, which published it without checking with me. I wrote a letter to the editor to complain about unequal treatment but there was no apology. I took these accusations seriously and sued the civil servant for defamation. Not surprisingly, the official recanted on the day of the hearing, and I was completely vindicated.

When my two-year term as special advisor to Stella Sigcau came to an end, I recommended my friend and colleague Mashudu Munyai as my successor and he was appointed.

◆

In 2003, the broad-based Black Economic Empowerment Act was promulgated, the main aim of which was to promote greater participation of historically disadvantaged black people in the mainstream economy of the country. It was an attempt to remedy the past.

Sadly, it has had mixed success, with extensive and pervasive corruption over the years under its guise. Equally sadly, too many black people remain trapped in poverty, and the future for them looks bleak. Likewise, too many white folk refuse to acknowledge and accept that they were the main beneficiaries of apartheid and colonialism. They cling to their power and privileges while they must know that change is inevitable. What they don't seem to understand is that they're harming the very self-interests they're trying so hard to protect – in the long term, a society that's characterised by such deep divisions isn't sustainable.

During the Mandela administration I'd been inspired, and during the Mbeki administration (1999-2008) I remained hopeful. But the Zuma administration (2009-2018) was an unmitigated disaster. As we all know from the revelations at the Zondo Commission, during that time corruption became firmly rooted in both the public and private sectors. This corruption has seriously undermined the gains that might otherwise have been achieved and has severely stunted economic growth. Money that should have gone towards improving the lives of our people has been used to fund the lavish lifestyles of politicians and businessmen alike. What has happened to the promise of a better life for all? Think of the positive impact we could have made on the lives of our people if we'd deployed the stolen billions of rands for education, housing or health and welfare, for example. It's such a shame.

The pursuit of wealth by whatever means necessary is truly a national disgrace and all those who enriched themselves through corrupt activities ought to be ashamed of themselves. The culprits are yet to be sanctioned, and until and unless this happens, the corruption will continue unabated. Many of those who've been implicated in the revelations at the commission should ultimately be held accountable. Hopefully, some of them might even go to jail.

I'm reminded of the largely successful Mandela and Mbeki administrations, and of my own generation, those stalwarts I had the pleasure and privilege of working with during the early days of Abasa, BMF and BLA. They were selfless leaders who worked tirelessly to improve the lives of not only their members but society in general. Those memories are what give me hope.

Eradicating apartheid was the best thing that could have happened for the country but it required a long and painful struggle and we must never forget the sacrifices, including the ultimate sacrifice of life, that so many of our people made so that we may enjoy the freedom we have today. Although wealth is still very much concentrated in the hands of our white counterparts, there is a very strong black middle class who are well educated, have good jobs, live in affluent suburbs and generally enjoy a very comfortable lifestyle.

Unless all of us, black and white alike, embrace change and work tirelessly towards economic and social justice, something will have to give and the consequences will be disastrous.

◆

I believe that the best way to safeguard the future is to ensure a brighter future for the latent talent in the townships, but the youth of today face many challenges, the biggest being finding suitable employment. When I look at the high level of unemployment among young people, it pains me no end. Just take a drive through any township at any time of the day and you'll see hundreds of young people aimlessly wandering around or standing by idly on street corners.

The official unemployment rate among those aged 15 to 34 was 46.3 percent at the beginning of 2021. Of these, over half had education levels below matric; a scant two percent were graduates and just 7.5 percent had tertiary qualifications. So life for the youth is a daily struggle for survival.

In these circumstances, it's incredibly difficult to motivate and inspire the youth. However, it's important for them not to succumb to despair, and to remain positive and alert to any opportunities that still arise, even under these dire circumstances. Above all, we need to remain patient and positive, and avoid frustration and anger, which lead into the mud, and destructive behaviour. My central philosophy is that no matter how hard the road, we must believe in the inherent good nature of people.

Values and principles are about how we're grounded. As the proverb says, when the roots of a tree decay, the branches die. Throughout my career, fundamental to my achievements has always been remaining true to who I am, standing firm on my values, principles and ethics, and remembering my roots.

My grandmother instilled her values in me from a very young age – humility, the value of hard work, discipline, perseverance, honesty, and respect and caring for others. Whenever I strayed, she would give me a stern and quizzical look and I knew instinctively that I needed to correct my behaviour. (My experience suggests that these are aspirational values, as human beings are frail by nature and we often falter. However, the most important thing is to learn from our mistakes and get back to basics.)

I honestly believe that great things can be achieved through hard work and determination. It's all about sowing and reaping – what you put in is what you will get out. Sow good, and good will come your way; bless others, and you'll be blessed. Most importantly, never be afraid – even to make mistakes. Mistakes often lead to life's greatest learning opportunities!

I've never been fearful of anything, and it is the fearlessness in my life that has underpinned my vision and drive to succeed. For me, success meant being able to travel and see the world, learn and better myself through study, experience and opportunities to ultimately be in a position where I could give back, because I have received so much.

14

THOUGHTS AT 70 AND BEYOND

In February 2020 I reached the magical age of 70 years – the biblical 'three-score and ten' that once marked the life expectancy
of a human.

Then came March, and with it the covid-19 pandemic, unprecedented in our lifetime. The government imposed a hard lockdown
that severely restricted our movements and confined most of us
to our homes. One of the unexpected benefits of this was that it
forced most of us, other than those involved in essential services,
to slow down quite dramatically. I was one of those who suddenly
found that I had more time for reading, thinking and reflecting. As
I looked back on my life, my family and my friends, I realised for
the first time just how far I've travelled over the years.

For anyone to reach the age of 70 is a huge blessing, and for me,
who lost so many friends and two brothers when they were young,
one of the big questions I have is why I've lived for so long while
others' lives ended so tragically and so soon.

The lockdown and the much slower pace also provided me the
valuable space to think about how I'd like to spend the rest of my
life. It is a fact that the years ahead of me are much shorter than the
years behind me. I ask myself questions like, how would I like to
be remembered? Will I leave this world a slightly better place than I
found it? Will I be able to say that my life was worthwhile?

I know this much is true: post-covid-19, I do not wish to return to the hectic world of work. I'm often asked how I balanced work and family life. Work-life balance is probably one of the most difficult tasks for any professional, and more so for a working parent and spouse. My approach is based on the old-fashioned (some may say conservative) precept that as a man and husband, my first priority has always been the well-being of my family.

But pursuing a career does require trade-offs and sacrifices, and my biggest regret is not having been able to spend more time with my children as they were growing up. It saddens me immensely that my relationship with my wife Amy has been strained for a number of years. We have decided to call it a day and are in the midst of divorce proceedings. We have endured so much hardship and crossed so many rivers together that I will always have her best interests at heart. My own happiness is inextricably bound to our children and our grandchildren – our daughter Althea has two daughters, Boitumelo and Tsholofelo; Cheryl has a pair of twins, a son, Zac and a daughter, Skylar, and a younger daughter, Jenna. Our son Alvin is still single.

Thankfully, today my grownup children tell me that now that they have children of their own, they have a clearer and better understanding of the challenges I encountered in maintaining the right balance.

That said, going forward, I'd like to make some meaningful lifestyle changes that will allow me to spend more quality time with family and friends. Although I still manage Uranus on a full-time basis, I'm now preparing Althea as my successor. I recognise and accept that it's time to slow down. I'd like to have more time to read and write – I already have a significant library of interesting books on my Kindle and I can't wait to get started! And I'd also like to have more time to play golf on the magnificent golf courses we're blessed to have in this country.

◆

'To understand the universe at the deepest level, we need to know not only how the universe behaves, but why.'

This is an upfront statement in the book *The Grand Design* by physicists Leonard Mlodinow and Stephen Hawking, leading to questions such as why is there something rather than nothing? Why do we exist? Why this particular set of laws and not some other?

I remember pondering questions like this from about age 12 as I looked up to the sky. I asked my mother, grandmother, uncles, aunts, teachers and even strangers for answers. Their responses were mainly blank stares and frowns of the 'you're too young to under-stand' variety. The best that was offered was the biblical version described in Genesis: 'All of this is God's creation', done so that mankind may praise and worship him and thereby benefit by living happily in the life hereafter. Not entirely satisfactory, I'm afraid.

What I now know is that these questions have been pondered over the ages by great minds, including biblical scholars, poets and philosophers, who have come up short. In the view of authors Mlodinow and Hawking, 'scientists have become the bearers of the torch of discovery in the quest for knowledge'.

Thanks to science, we now know how the universe started with the 'big bang' some 13,7 billion years ago. We know the universe is expanding, and that the expansion rate is slowing down. We know that our sun is but one of over 200 billion stars in the universe. We know that neither our solar system nor our planet is at the centre of the universe. We know that our sun will eventually – a few billion years in the future – die. We also know that the planet was only suitable for life as we know it when the universe was at least 10 billion years old. God is indeed patient!

Thanks to my reading, I've been aware for a while now that we live on a planet that appears finely tuned for our existence – it's a 'goldilocks' planet, with conditions 'just right', neither too hot nor too cold, for humans to live and thrive on it. What's new to me is that science has shown that the entire universe appears to be finely tuned, which means that if the universe were only slightly different, then we couldn't exist. Inevitably, the authors ask, 'What are we to make of this fine tuning? Is it evidence that the universe, after all, was designed by a benevolent creator? Or does science offer another explanation?' And they answer this question by saying, 'The universe can and will create itself from nothing. Spontaneous creation is the reason there is something rather than nothing, why the universe exists, why we exist. It is not necessary to invoke God to light the blue torch paper and set the universe going.'

As I was reflecting on all of this recently, I spoke to a good friend about life in general. We spoke about God – who or what is God? If we see God as a higher consciousness, then God is truly omnipotent and omniscient – in lay terms, having great power and influence and knowing everything.

I'm grateful for my gifts although I confess that at times I'm envious of those around me who were born with the gift of faith – people who live simple lives, in the moment, with no care about tomorrow. They believe that they don't have to worry about anything or anyone because God will take care of them; God shoulders all the blame and responsibility for the bad that happens to them and deserves all the praise and glory for the good. And when they die they will go to heaven and live happily ever after.

This friend and I spoke about the life hereafter and agreed that as spiritual beings we're not confined to this tiny planet in this tiny solar system, but that the vast and infinite universe is where we will most likely roam. Only our tiny minds perceive this life of ours on this planet as somehow our ultimate destiny.

Given that our entire solar system is like a speck of dust in the universe, it's hard to imagine that our lives have some higher purpose. But who knows? All I know is that I have to make the best of my life while I can. I have to make the best of the gifts I was born with. I have to live not just for myself but for others too.

Poet Maya Angelou aptly captured what I've always believed when she wrote in her 1993 book *Wouldn't Take Nothing for my Journey Now*, 'It is this belief in a power larger than myself and other than myself, which allows me to venture into the unknown and even the unknowable.'

AFTERWORD

In July 2021, when I was travelling with Jeff van Rooyen to CMR
Golf Club for a meeting, along the way he stopped and bought a
bag of pies and drinks, which he distributed to the caddies at the
club when he arrived. He later provided transport money to assist
them getting home. He acted in a similar way when we went to the
Country Club Johannesburg.

On another occasion we went for a walk in Alexandra and again
he gave money for food to youngsters who were just sitting around.
When walking in Riverlea several women came out of their homes
to say hello, and he greeted all with the same warmth and dignity.
You would have thought he was a football star – they're so proud of
how one of their own had successfully emerged from their streets.

In this book, you've read about Jeff's amazing successes as a high-
powered businessman who's climbed the corporate ladder – how
he emerged from the townships and the challenges he faced to be
educated in apartheid South Africa.

But who is Jeff the man? Getting together with Jeff's business
associates, friends, golf partners (Norman Mbazima and Thabo
Khunyeli), family (wife Amy, daughters Althea and Cheryl, son
Alvin, and grandchildren Zac, Skylar, Jenna, Boitumelo and
Tsholofelo), a picture emerges that's very different from what you
may expect, and it's what makes Jeff so interesting.

Jeff had to fight his way out of the townships and enter a white man's world, and he became one of only four black (African and coloured) chartered accountants countrywide in 1981. Having arrived in a more comfortable and secure world, you might have expected him to stay in this new comfort zone. But that just isn't Jeff. He didn't stay put, as this book has shown.

Jeff is a warm, friendly individual. He's also restless and thrives on new challenges – he is persistent and he questions everything. His business associates jokingly describe him as 'naughty in a good way'. Although he's soft-spoken, he participates strongly and can be very direct. Very diligent and always well prepared, Jeff follows through: he returns calls, and he's not afraid to challenge his colleagues on the board if necessary. He's honest and transparent, and he listens well.

Jeff is someone who engages with adversaries in a calm and dignified manner even in the face of provocation, and he tends to get the upper hand in tough situations, possibly because he doesn't shy away, nor does he take things for granted. He's a doer, not waiting for others to do the work.

In the boardroom he's strong on etiquette, and he's not scared to put forward his views in a respectful way. As chairman, he calls board members to order when required but he also ensures that everyone's voice is heard. Although members of the board have distinct opinions, Jeff will try and get them on track. His philosophy is to work hard but have lots of fun, and he's available any time to discuss issues.

At the end of the day board members are paid to be honest and transparent, and Jeff has grappled with adversity and disagreeable people. Sadly, not all disagreements lend themselves to amicable solutions. As a result, he's not shy about engaging lawyers and going to court.

But Jeff is also highly reflective and willing to change his view – he's a strategist who doesn't interrupt or get into slanging matches. In the end, though, the majority rules, whatever his personal opinion, and after the board meeting it's just one big family, however challenging, and there are no recriminations.

Jeff has his own set of values and principles. The mark of a good leader is to know right from wrong, and if something is unfair, he won't let it go. Furthermore, he's agile in the business world, doesn't align himself with factions, and moves with the times. But he's also prepared to walk away from deals, irrespective of the potential profit, if there's no synergy and value alignment. In this, he says he likes 'reading the tea leaves', which means considering all the information before trying to predict the outcome.

Unsurprisingly, he's philanthropic and community-oriented, and deeply affected by stories of woe and misfortune. He's always had the desire to help those less fortunate than himself, and enjoys helping others reach their potential. Few quietly give back the way he does.

Jeff has contributed in many spheres: uplifting black entrepreneurs, the formation of Abasa, and numerous interventions in the township, from quietly supporting children struggling to pay school fees, to buying a vehicle to transport Riverlea youngsters to athletics meetings, providing uniforms and launching a campaign to highlight the dangers of hookah pipes. In return, he's received a remarkable response from members of the community.

He set up the Riverlea Development Trust to respond to the needs of the community. He also set up groups of women sewing school uniforms, took groups of young people from Riverlea and neighbouring townships to Pick n Pay's head office in Bedfordview to be screened for jobs, and established or involved himself in a range of other income-generating projects.

At Uranus Investment Holdings, his own company, he brought on board folk from Riverlea and neighbouring townships as black economic empowerment partners. They became investors and board members, and he's created considerable value for them over the years. They remain invested in Uranus to this day.

Despite all of this, he is humble and understated. His office is quite modest, with his favourite pictures being drawings by the children of a school with profound disabilities he helps to fund. His home is modestly furnished, with no substantial trappings or paintings and plush carpets. It's just a normal, functional and comfortable home.

Jeff was very strict with his kids, and both his daughters Cheryl and Althea blamed their dad for not being there during their schooling, as he was always working or away travelling, and their mom Amy had to bring them up. As they got older and had children of their own this all changed, and they understood his sacrifices so that they could have a better life. In fact, his daughter Cheryl informed him growing up that she never wanted to be like him, and now, since having children of her own, she wants to be just like him!

Althea, who's just joined Uranus, feels that Jeff is far too generous and says she must sometimes pull him back and tell him to say 'no'. She prefers the technique of giving people something to fish with instead of giving them fish. An example of this is, following a profitable exit from a Uranus investment in 2019, Jeff provided all his staff with home loans.

Jeff's grandchildren really love him – he's fun and generous, plays games like chess with them, engages with them as young adults on worldly topics and gives them respect.

Jeff's experiences enable him to see things in a different way. He's walked a longer journey than most in coming from a place of deprivation, social imprisonment and poverty. He's conscious of his story of triumph over adversity, when so many fall short of their potential, and of apartheid's message that 'you're not good enough' based on the colour of your skin. Jeff's biggest challenge was to shake off those shackles, and not to believe what others perceived to be his weaknesses – and throughout his life, he's managed to breach those constraints.

Barry Cohen
Cape Town, March 2022

REFERENCES AND FURTHER READING

Ackerman, R and Prichard, D. 2004. *Hearing Grasshoppers Jump.* David Philip Publishers.

Angelou, M. 1994. *Wouldn't Take Nothing for my Journey Now.* Bantam.

Baldwin, J. 1963. *The Fire Next Time.* Dial Press.

Gracian, B and Maurer, C. 1992. *The Art of Worldly Wisdom: A Pocket Oracle.* Doubleday.

Hawking, S and Mlodinow, L. 2010. *The Grand Design.* Bantam.

Heatlie, D. 2019. 'They stood their ground! – Professional gangsters in South African Indian Society, 1940-1970'. Thesis. University of the Witwatersrand.

It's My Life ... RoziefromJozie. 1 May 2006. 'The Gangs of Jo'burg ... 70s and 80s'. https://rosemarie64.blogspot.com/2006/05/gangs-of-joburg-70s-and-80s.html

Khaya Volunteer Projects. n.d. 'Township Life in South Africa – A volunteer's perspective'. http://www.khayavolunteer.com/news/180-township-life-in

Kings, S. 22 February 2013. 'Gold dust cripples Riverlea'. *Mail&Guardian.* https://mg.co.za article/2013-02-22-00-gold-dust-cripples-riverlea/

McFarlane's New Africa News Service. n.d. USA.

National Institute for Occupational Health. 2018. 'Working Conditions and Health Outcomes of Caddies Working in Golf Courses in the City of Johannesburg'. https://www.nioh.ac.za/wp-content/uploads/2019/08/Caddy-Report-Approved-Final.pdf

Nieftagodien, N and Bonner, P. 2008. *Alexandra: A History*. Wits University Press.

Observation Mission to the USA. Brochure, October 1990.

Raffy. 22 October 2009. 'Riverlea'. Growing Up In Riverlea. https://growingupinriverlea.blogspot.com/

World Health Organization. n.d. 'The Health, Environment Development Study – Preliminary Results from Phase One, 2006'. Research Report.

APPENDIX I: PRESIDENTS OF ABASA

I was elected the founding president of Abasa in 1985. One of my closest friends, Willie Ramoshaba, was elected vice-president. Freelance journalist Mashudu Ramano was appointed executive director. Other founding members were Israel Skosana, Jeff Rapoo, Jay Pema, Younaid Waja, Moses Sindane and Verney Mathabatha. Soon thereafter Juneas Lekgetha, Moses Kgosana, Sizwe Nxasana, Sathie Gounden, Lloyd Theunissen, Andre de Wet and Ken Nomlala joined the organisation.

Presidents of Abasa:

NAME	PERIOD
Jeff van Rooyen	1985-1990
Israel Skosana	1990-1992
Juneas Lekgetha	1992-1995
Sizwe Nxasana	1995-1998
Moses Kgosana	1998-2000
Sathie Gounden	2000-2002
Futhi Mtoba	2002-2004
Avhashoni Ramikosi*	2004-2006
Victor Sekese	2006-2008
Tsakani Maluleke	2008-2010
Lwazi Bam	2010-2011
Andile Khumalo	2011-2013
Tantaswa Fubu	2013-2015
Gugu Ncube	2015-2018

NAME	PERIOD
Mbusiswa Ngcobo*	2018-2018
Ashley Dicken	2018-2021
Linda Maqoma	2021-

* Avhashoni Ramikosi was implicated in the VBS Mutual Bank fraud and the case is still pending. His membership of Abasa will be reviewed once the matter is settled. Mbusiswa Ngcobo was involved in a legal dispute with Abasa during his tenure as president and was removed from his position and as a member of Abasa.

APPENDIX II: AWARDS AND CITATIONS

- National outstanding mentor award from the Association of Black Accountants of South Africa, 26 November 1987, in recognition of 'consistent support to the association and contribution to the accountancy profession'.

- Award from the Chartered Accountants Eden Trust, 1988, 'in recognition of your valued contribution'.

- Special recognition award from the National Association of Black Accountants (USA), 30 June 1990, 'in recognition of outstanding achievement in the accounting profession'.

- Scroll from the University of South Africa, faculty of economic and management sciences, November 1993, 'In appreciation of services rendered with conspicuous dedication and enthusiasm to the community of chartered accountants in South Africa'.

- Award from the Association for the Advancement of Black Accountants of Southern Africa, 1995, 'In recognition of your valued contribution'.

- Title of 'Professor Extraordinarius' from the University of South Africa, 2001.

- Achievement award from the University of Pretoria, school of public management and administration, 19 November 2004, 'For longstanding dedicated services in nation building, public and private sector financial services to South Africa and international community'.

- Award from the Public Accountants and Auditors Board, 22 November 2005, 'In recognition of his dedicated service as a member of the Board from 1991 to 1996 and from 2001 to 2004 and as chairman during 1995'.

- 25th Anniversary Achievement Award from the Association for the Advancement of Black Accountants of Southern Africa, 2010, 'for your contribution to Abasa's legacy 1985–1990'.

- Honorary life membership of the South African Institute of Chartered Accountants, 25 April 2013, 'as evidence of appreciation of contributions made to the accountancy profession in South Africa'.

- Inyathelo Philanthropy Award from the South African Institute for Advancement, 5 November 2013, 'in recognition of leadership and excellence in personal South African philanthropy'.

- 35th Anniversary Full Circle Award from the Association for the Advancement of Black Accountants of Southern Africa, 2020.

APPENDIX III: BUSINESS LESSONS LEARNED

As a non-executive director of three listed companies over a period of 15 years, I've had to deal with my fair share of boardroom politics and power struggles.

All directors have a fiduciary duty to the company. This means that directors are obliged to put the interests of the company above their own. Sadly, this is not always the case. Boards are made up of some powerful people with strong characters and huge egos. While most boards function reasonably well, directors are also human and subject to human frailty. Some people may think that they're always the smartest in the room, while others have an inflated sense of their own importance. Some tend to be poor listeners and sometimes push ill-considered views very hard; they sulk and behave disruptively if they don't get their way.

I've had to call time-out in meetings on a number of occasions to allow tempers to cool and emotions to settle. Despite disruptive behaviour, you still have to get through the agenda of the day and ensure the best possible outcome for the business. Robust debate is essential and must be encouraged, as it enhances the quality of decision-making. However, the debate has to take place within the context of basic decency and decorum, and on the basis of mutual trust and respect.

In recent times we've seen some boardroom squabbles in listed companies spill out into the public domain. In my view this is unfortunate and hardly inspires confidence in the conduct of boards as a whole. If we take our duties and responsibilities as directors seriously, we should do our best to contain our differences to within the boardroom. The boardroom is like the bedroom: don't kiss and tell!

Here are my thoughts on the business environment, the management and control environment, and the board of directors.

The business environment

Businesses are growing in size and complexity. For example, Pick n Pay has an annual turnover of R90 billion. The group moves an unbelievably huge volume of goods, including general merchandise, clothing and groceries, from suppliers to warehouses and stores. The group has also expanded into financial services, and customers are able draw cash and pay bills at the tills. The group also recently acquired a licence as a mobile virtual network operator, which means you can now get a PnP SIM card for your mobile phone.

All businesses I've been involved with are expanding their footprint across Africa. There's no room for complacency. Complacency leads to stagnation. Businesses are always searching for new growth opportunities.

Some businesses have to reinvent themselves otherwise they may cease to exist. For example, MTN built a massive telecommunications network and their main business was providing connectivity. Today, through mobile money, they're big in financial services. They're also building a significant media-services business, providing music and entertainment content. Exxaro is reinventing itself and looking at a future beyond coal due to climate change. The company aims to build a business at scale in renewable energy over the next seven to 10 years.

There are always unexpected challenges, such as the financial crisis of 2009 and the recent covid-19 pandemic. Companies must build strength and resilience to get through crises, for example, by trimming cost structures and preserving cash by delaying shareholder dividends.

The management and control environment

Boards must ensure that they appoint the right chief executive officer (CEO) who not only has the required knowledge, skills and experience but also strong leadership skills.

Equally important, management must be seen to embrace the values and principles of the company. There are myriad examples over the last few years of unethical behaviour which has resulted in massive value destruction for all stakeholders.

The board must allow the CEO the space to build his own team – after all, the CEO is held accountable for the performance and results of the business.

The board must also appoint the right chief financial officer (CFO). If there's collusion between the CEO and the CFO, it spells disaster for the business. If the board can't trust either the CEO or CFO, they should not be appointed.

The board must appoint the right external auditors, and must ensure that there's a strong internal audit and risk-management function.

The board of directors

The chairman is like the conductor of a huge orchestra. The chairman must have basic knowledge, skill and experience in fields such as business, finance and corporate governance. In addition, they must have strong leadership skills, sound values and principles, an ability to work with people across racial and gender barriers, an ability to recognise and harness the strengths of fellow board members, and an ability to make the tough calls when necessary without fear or favour.

The chairman must ensure that the board has the appropriate skills mix, for example, corporate governance, renewable energy, climate change and sustainability, innovation and technology, finance, legal and the relevant industry experience. Some of the skills that may not be readily available may be insourced.

Other lessons learned

I've learned some valuable lessons along my journey from the townships to the boardrooms of JSE-listed companies. I feel privileged be able to share some of the ideas that have worked for me, although these aren't exhaustive or in any particular order of importance.

We live in a moral universe. Martin Luther King Jnr said, 'We shall overcome because the arc of the moral universe is long but it bends towards justice.' This is a very profound statement, given all the evil that is so prevalent in the world today. We tend to look at events from the perspective of our own lifespan which, in most cases, is less than 100 years. We must learn to take a much longer, multigenerational view. For example, there was no justice for many who were born into slavery and died as slaves. The same is true for those who lived and died under apartheid. Thankfully, while I was born into apartheid, I've lived to see the end of it. I'm unlikely to live to see the end of economic and social injustice, not only in this country but around the world. However, I have faith that day, too, will surely come.

Talent is equally dispersed across race, gender and geography. Don't be concerned about the accident of your birth. Discover your talent and make the most of it.

Learn from the past but don't remain trapped in the past. You won't recognise opportunity if you remain trapped in the past. Unshackle your body and mind, and embrace change.

Learn from failure and don't make any excuses. Take responsibility, hold yourself accountable, and try to do better the next time.

You can learn from anyone, regardless of their background or social status. You do yourself a disservice if you think you can only learn from the rich and powerful.

Don't allow anyone to define what you can or can't do. You know yourself better than anyone else does. So the only person who knows your limitations is the one you see when you look in a mirror.

Aspire to be authentic. Avoid pretence. Be who you are and you'll draw kindred spirits towards you.

Have a grateful spirit and remember that greed is insatiable.

Have a sense of humour. See the funny side of things and laugh out loud.

Don't be a bearer of bad news. Rather share the good news when you come across it.

Try to see the good in people and you may be pleasantly surprised.

Be sensitive to the needs of the less fortunate. You don't get to where you are without help from others, so pay it forward.

Don't judge other people because you aren't walking in their shoes. It's far better to have empathy and try to be helpful if you're in a position to do so.

The darkest hour is before the dawn. Regardless of the challenges you might be facing at a particular time, always remain hopeful and have faith that tomorrow will be better.

You get what you work for and not necessarily what you deserve. You may deserve success but there are countless deserving people who end up nowhere. It's better to step up and work for what you want.

Cultivate good habits. Cultivate a good work ethic. Aspire to be knowledgeable, reliable, conscientious and trustworthy.

Stand up for your beliefs. This is a hard thing to do and often comes at a cost but it's worthwhile.

Nobody can read your mind. You may think what you like and be safe. Keep a tight rein on your emotions and be careful of what you say.

Unless you're alert, you won't see the opportunities around you. As soon as you have the awareness, seize the moment.

You're smarter and tougher than you think. Believe in yourself and step out of your comfort zone.

Avoid misery by choosing your battles. Don't be prepared to die on every hill.

Always remain calm in the face of adversity. This will help you find the solution more easily.

Exceptional leaders have a higher-than-normal pain threshold. The higher the pain threshold, the higher the risk – and the reward.

Always treat everyone with respect and don't discriminate on any basis.

You don't always have to have the last word. Stop speaking when you've made your point.

Speak less, listen more. Sharpen your observation and listening skills. It's the best way to learn.

Be kind. A kind word or gesture towards others will brighten lives in ways that may surprise you.

Health is more precious than wealth. If your health fails, you can't buy it back even if you have all the money in the world.

Have patience. Certain events have their own momentum. Allow them to unfold in their own time.

APPENDIX IV: THE PLIGHT OF THE
TOWNSHIPS

Sadly, since my childhood in Riverlea and Alexandra, life has become much worse for the residents of these places.

Despite a number of 'renewal projects' in Alexandra over the years, including the R1,3-billion seven-year redevelopment plan announced by President Mbeki in 2001, the quality of life for the people of this township has worsened. The population has more than quadrupled since my childhood. All those wonderful spaces that we used to play in have disappeared. Houses of poor quality have been built everywhere. Instead of spacious yards, you now have to move through narrow corridors to get from one house to the next. There's massive overcrowding, and because there is no space for horizontal extensions to the houses, the trend these days is for people to build double storeys.

The situation in Riverlea is similar, and these challenges exist in many townships across the country.

As I reflect on where the people of Riverlea and Alexandra come from, where they are today and what the future holds for them, it becomes clear that without significant government intervention in housing, education and health and welfare services, the future looks bleak. The private sector also has a vital role to play in job creation and skills development.

I think of what President Nelson Mandela said prior to our first democratic elections – that 'each of us' would have a right to exercise a choice, and that that choice would determine our socioeconomic future and that of our children. 'Join us in the patriotic endeavour to ensure that all our people share in that future,' he said. Note that Mandela said all of our people, not some of our people.

These challenges aren't insurmountable. The government needs to have the will to catalyse change by working in partnership with business and civil society. We must stop squandering our limited resources and deploy the vast knowledge, skill and experience we have to execute the grand plans that we've designed over the years. Such interventions will put South Africa's townships on a positive trajectory for the future.

It can be done.